Endorsem

From Victoria's introductic........................ was captivated and my heart was touched! You will feel as if Victoria is sitting there with you, speaking encouraging, loving, life-giving words that will inspire and encourage you. What a sweet breath of love and acceptance poured over me as I read each page. I felt such refreshment and relaxation.

As a gifted author, Victoria is authentic, and her words come from her obvious deep and intimate relationship with her heavenly Father. She knows His heart and has been able to capture on paper His love for you, His dearly treasured daughter.

Grab your coffee, tea or lemonade, because experiencing this book is truly the same as receiving personal, individual letters, or chatting across a café table. Dear You is beneficial for every teen girl to read, as well as women of any age that struggle with her identity, self worth, and truly knowing how her heavenly Father sees her. This book is not only perfect for individual study, but as a group study for women to share together as they build up one another up as Daughters of the King.

—LaJuan (56), wife and homeschooling mother

Dear You is a book that has the potential to change your life. The content feeds your soul to know you are loved, and the chapter questions help you discover who Yeshua designed you to be so you can live out your calling with no negative programing holding you back. A must-study book for every woman seeking to thrive spiritually.

—Melanie (26), author

As soon as I began reading this book, peace and joy flooded my heart. It was as if Victoria was talking straight to me. Her words were exactly what I needed to hear at that moment and she opened my eyes. She reminds us that we are all beautifully and wonderfully made and not to compare ourselves to others. As I was growing up, I always thought that I was not as pretty as all the other girls. I thought that the girls would not like me just because of the way I looked or talked. It can be really hard, but Victoria reminds us that we are not alone and that we have people we can reach out to for help who want to make this journey with us. Through everything, we know that Adonai will always be there for us and that He will never forsake us even in our hardest times. I believe with all my heart that this book will be a great blessing to ladies of all ages. I'm encouraging all of my friends to read it!

—Joy (19), student

Dear You

Letters of Identity in Yeshua
— FOR WOMEN —

Victoria Humphrey

Lederer Books
A division of
Messianic Jewish Publishers
Clarksville, MD 21029

Printed in the United States of America

Cover photo taken by Hannah Jean Photography

Cover & Graphic Design by Yvonne Vermillion,
Magic Graphix, Westfork, Arkansas

2019   1

ISBN 978-1-7339354-0-1

Library of Congress Control Number: 2019939239

Published by:
Lederer Books
A Division of Messianic Jewish Publishers & Resources
6120 Day Long Lane
Clarksville, MD 21029

Distributed by:
Messianic Jewish Publishers & Resources
Order line: (800) 410-7367
lederer@messianicjewish.net
www.MessianicJewish.net

To all the daughters of Adonai:
You are so beloved by Him.

Contents

And this is my prayer: that your love may more and more overflow in fullness of knowledge and depth of discernment, so that you will be able to determine what is best and thus be pure and without blame for the Day of Messiah, filled with the fruit of righteousness that comes through Yeshua the Messiah-to the glory and praise of God.

PHILIPPIANS 1:9-11

Preface

To me, nothing says "I'm here for you" more than a letter in my mailbox.

I grew up in an era prior to emails, when pen-pals were the greatest craze. Perhaps I found my love for writing then, at the tender age of eight. Letter-writing was a staple of my childhood. I had nearly one hundred pen-pals I feverishly wrote to one summer, and there was nothing more delightful than to find an envelope in the mailbox with my name scrawled along its front.

It made me feel important. Loved.

Three o'clock was the happiest hour of my childhood, when the mail truck would slowly work its way down our street as I peeped out through my second-floor bedroom window. The mature maples that lined the road could never muffle that old, familiar sound. I could hear the truck coming from two streets over, my ears tuned to the soft puttering. As soon as the truck started to pull away from our driveway towards the next-door neighbor's, I was already out the door running to see what was left behind.

I never knew what treasures I'd find.

Still, as an adult, the mail is always a highlight—and if there are no letters, a disappointment—of my day. Although I don't have nearly as many pen-pals as I had when I was young, I still send out notes to friends whenever I can. I like to think that other people enjoy getting mail as much as I do, that their eyes will light up at an envelope with their name hand written on its front in the midst of type-faced bills and junk mail bearing the impersonal "Current Resident."

I guess you could say letters are my love language.

Maybe I'm just a crazy letter lady, but deep down I believe I'm not the only one. We all want to feel appreciated. We all want to be told that we have potential. In my case, maybe the letter bug is hereditary. My grandma truly is a letter-writing legend, typing thousands of missives on her typewriter. A note from Grandma was always special, and not just because of the quirky vintage type that marched across the page. She always had a word of praise or encouragement, and occasionally a gentle admonishment. She sent letters to family members, missionaries, and countless strangers who had become her friends. She had a knack for tracking down an address, always being sure that you knew you were important to her.

That is what I hope this book is to you.

If I had your address and a never-ending supply of postage stamps, I'd send you a letter, too. I'd want you to know that I'm here for you. I care about you. I'd want you to know just how amazing you are, with all of your quirks and graces, your past and your future. I'd want to connect you with so many brave young women just like you, who share your same struggles and fears, the same bold faith and courageous heart. I'd want to show you that you're not alone, that you have an army of sisters who are marching forward with you.

I'd want you to find the treasure of how Adonai sees you.

You are so adored, so cherished, so perfectly equipped by the King of Heaven, the *Melech*[1] who rules your heart. More than my words in your mailbox, I'd want you to see His love letter written on the pages of Scripture—not just to a generation, or a people, or a place in history...but a love letter, directed to you.

You, His beloved.

There are so many things I want you to know, so many Scriptures I want you to behold. Nevertheless, the truth is that I don't have your address, and if I did, I don't have an unending stamp supply.

But I'm not giving up.

No, I'm not giving up on reaching out to you, precious sister who is bought and redeemed. Consider this book my attempt to send you a package filled with letters, straight from my heart—and Yeshua's—to yours.

From my mailbox to yours,

Victoria Humphrey

---

1. "King" in Hebrew

Introduction

Dear You,

Yes, you—the amazing person that you are, reading my words right now. Maybe you're reading this curled up in your favorite well-worn armchair with a mug of tea, or maybe you're relaxing at the beach as the waves dance and splash on your toes. Maybe you're reading this spread out on a blanket under a canopy of the brightest stars, all of heaven shining down upon you. Maybe you're sitting in a quaint little coffee shop over a steaming latte, or maybe you're on a quiet bench at the park while squirrels scurry around as your companions. Maybe you're sitting on the creaking back porch swing, surrounded by wiry Queen Anne's lace and a plethora of potted petunias while the sky turns gold with the sinking sun—

Which is where I am, writing to you.

Wherever you are, however you're reading this, there is one thing I want to shout loud and clear right at the get-go:

The fact that you are reading this book is not an accident.

I wrote this book with you in mind. I know it's hard to believe, but it's the truth. Perhaps I've never met you in person, or never had the opportunity to cross oceans and climb mountains to share our hearts around the kitchen table. Perhaps I've met you once or twice, but you've never shared with me the whole story of your life that I long to hear. Perhaps we're even close friends, and we've even talked excitedly about how Adonai is moving in our lives, but you still struggle to grab hold of the abundant life that Yeshua offers.[1]

I may or may not know you personally, but every word I've written in these pages is drenched in prayer for *you*. Prayer that these words would touch you, change you, and free you to be all that you can be. Prayer that you would receive these words with all the love with which they were written, prayer that you would flourish in the love of Adonai.

The words I've written, they're the truth about your identity.

I know you're going to shy away from it. You're going to squirm and think of the lies the enemy spews concerning who you are instead. You're going to want to fall comfortably into the doubts and fears and chains that hold you back from being a bold woman who is confident in all Yeshua has said and done.

In the name and power of Yeshua HaMashiach, those chains have to fall.

You cannot say that the truths I'm about to present don't apply to you. You cannot say that you've made too many mistakes, or believe that you're too far gone to receive His love. You cannot choose to wallow in your past, to sink lower into the mire.

---

1.   John 10:10

You are redeemed. You are chosen. You are loved.[2]

In a world that demands airbrushed perfection, I know how hard it is to believe that you are enough. I know it's hard to believe in a name-brand, possession-saturated culture, that before the creation of the world, Adonai chose you to be His own, and you are worth every drop of blood spilled from the veins of His Son, Yeshua.[3] It's such a foreign concept, so hard to grasp and understand. A friend of mine once explained it in a way that changed my perspective forever, saying, "You wouldn't pay $50,000 for a $5,000 car. *Don't ever think that Adonai would pay the expensive price of the life of His Son for someone who wasn't worthy.*" It bears repeating, again and again, until it is so ingrained in our minds that all the lies flee:

You were worth every drop of blood spilled from the veins of Yeshua.[4]

You are not your past, your family baggage, or your unfortunate circumstances. You are washed clean in Yeshua,[5] and as such, it's time to walk in newness of life. Consider this book as a messenger from Adonai's heart to yours. He wants you to walk in the words of life between the covers of this book, to allow these chapters to stir your heart to what He says in Scripture. He wants you to not just *know*, but to *experience* that He is a good, good Father. He delights to give good gifts,[6] He delights over you in Heavenly song.[7]

---

2. 1 Peter 2:9
3. John 3:16-17
4. Ephesians 2:4-7
5. Isaiah 1:18
6. James 1:17
7. Zephaniah 3:17

I'm suggesting a paradigm shift.

Before you begin reading this book, recognize the lies of the enemy, and arm yourself to shoot those lies down with the truth of Adonai's promises. See yourself as worthy. Pray and partner with Yeshua to dismantle every scheme of the enemy to throw grenades into the battlefield of your mind.

Take every thought captive.[8]

Darkness and light have nothing in common,[9] just as fear and faith cannot coexist. You can't allow trashy lies into your mind and expect life-giving truth to come out. You can't be influenced by the comparison of lifestyles and histories, because *Adonai's promises* are who you are. These promises weren't just written for me, your sister, or your friends.

These are promises made by El Shaddai to YOU.

I grew up in the Messianic culture, which at times was tough. Because of it, my peers and I didn't fit in with the church, and at the same time we didn't fit in with the synagogue, either. Created for community, it's hard to stand alone. I noticed how my friends decided to splash in the shallow end where we could morph into whatever we wanted to whomever we wanted. In the shallow end, we don't touch the deep topics that separate us...but we don't grow, either. We ride the waves of our parents' faith, but we, ourselves, are void of power.

Adonai wants you to go deeper.

He wants you to jump into the deep end with both feet, to be immersed in His promises and Spirit. He wants to use you, to take you on your own wild adventure. He wants you to make those hard choices, to build your own firm foundation on Yeshua's love for you.[10]

8.   2 Corinthians 10:5
9.   2 Corinthians 6:14
10. 2 Timothy 2:19

Are you ready for the Creator of the galaxies to breathe into your heart?

This is the greatest adventure, my friend. Dear, amazing you—take hold of every page, soak it up like a sponge. Use this book as a tool to take you deeper. Look up every Scripture reference, and let His Word transform you from the inside out. Dig deep into your heart and apply yourself when answering the questions at the end of each chapter. Copy the banners from each chapter onto cardstock, color them out as you pray, and string them boldly across your room as visual reminders of who you are in Yeshua. Press into the words Adonai speaks over you, casting identity and vision for your life. Highlight this book, write in the margins, stain it with the remnants of your tears and coffee. Absorb Adonai's promises and inhale His love, because nothing can nullify this fact:

The King of all Creation is crazy about you.

And quite frankly, so am I. I'm standing here as your sister, cheering you on!

So let the journey begin.

CHAPTER ONE

You Are Forgiven

Dear Forgiven You,

There is no pit too deep for Adonai's hand to reach.

Your story may feel so broken that nothing could ever hold the pieces from crumbling out from under you, like you could never walk with head held high and crowned with joy.[1] You may think that you've gone too far, crossed the line too many times, and have outspent Adonai's ability to forgive. You may wonder if He could ever use you, knowing that there are so many other girls out there that fit a bill of perfection while you...well, you just feel perfectly soiled.

Through Yeshua, you can be washed clean—turning dirty rags into snow white linen.[2]

I know it's such a mind-boggling concept to grasp, the notion of a love so deep that it dies and gives everything to make you clean. This is so crucial for you to believe with all your soul, because from it stems the power to believe every promise Adonai has spoken over you in His love.

---

1. Isaiah 51:11
2. Isaiah 1:18

The cross of Yeshua is our gateway into this promise land.[3]

Just as the Israelites painted the blood over the doorframe of their homes before they marched out free,[4] it's the same way for us, too.[5] In order for us to march out free to take hold of all of our potential and worth and purpose, we have to realize the price, and the desperate need of cleansing for life anew.

Adonai cannot dwell among the impure. He can't have a relationship with those in sin.[6]

For generations, we sought atonement through the blood of bulls and goats, yet they could only cover the action of our offenses.[7] Their blood couldn't change our hearts, it couldn't wash away the desire and lust of sin from our minds.

Their blood could only cover, but Yeshua's blood seeps in.[8]

Adonai's love for you is so radical and His desire for you is so intense, that He willingly gives His Son to cleanse away your filth and bring you back into relationship with Him. He writes His law on your heart. He gets to the root of the problem as the permanent solution.[9]

Yeshua crosses all barriers—finite man and infinite Elohim, the highest sphere of heaven and the darkest place of death—all because of this love.

Never before in the history of humankind, and never again, will there ever be such a solution as the one Adonai gives by

3.   John 3:14
4.   Exodus 12:21-23
5.   1 Corinthians 5:7-8
6.   Ephesians 5:5
7.   Leviticus 16
8.   Hebrews 9:11-14
9.   Jeremiah 31:33

extending His Salvation—His Yeshua—as a way for us to dwell with Him within the veil.[10] He throws out a lifeline, a direct map to freedom, a way of cleansing to restore your soul. He provides a way and does everything possibly needed to bring you into covenant with Him...if only you'll accept.

How could we ever let our lack of self esteem (or rather, lack of belief in His truth) stand in our way of abundant life and blessing?

Here is the truth: Yeshua's ministry was not about confirming the spiritual elite in His day, but rather searching for hearts of desperate people longing for a beautiful change. He didn't come for the healthy, but for the sick.[11]

He came to pick up our pieces, and glue them back together again.

Whatever pieces you feel are broken on the floor, He's standing there waiting for you to ask Him to step in. He wants to kneel down in the middle of your mess and place each shard of glass into the mosaic He's creating with your life. Gorgeous, lovely mosaics can only be made from the shards of the broken. Vases, tea cups, decorative plates, it's only when they're smashed beyond recognition of their original identity that they can be formed into the greatest, most breathtaking masterpieces. Each smooth, sharp piece is no longer defined as what it used to be: a tea cup or your grandmother's china.

Now, it's defined as a work of art, an amazing collage designed with skill and purpose.

There is so much meaning here, and so much we can learn as we see that each part of our journey is being used

10. Hebrews 6:19
11. Mark 2:17

in the most beautiful way. There is no shard, no moment of time, being wasted as Yeshua steps in and rearranges each piece with such love into a glorious display of color and joy. We've been shattered, dying to sin, and regathered, belong to Messiah.[12] What sin has done to mar us, change us in the worst way possible, does not hold power over this fact:

In Yeshua, sin does not define us.

You are not your past mistakes or the secrets you've tried in vain to keep in the dark. You are not your family history or what once blemished your driving record. You have been freed from being yoked to sin, bought by Adonai with a price high above any monetary sum.[13] Yet, in this glorious story, there is one thing that can keep you from reaching the "Happily Ever After":

We all desire to be the one rescued by the Prince, but sometimes we become our own dragon, keeping us chained and captive.

We become our own worst enemies, refusing to walk out of our jail cell when Yeshua has turned the key and the door stands wide open. The Prince has come, our price was paid, and oh what a beautiful wedding is just around the corner! Like a Bridegroom, His heart is pulsing with hope, racing at the thought of being with you.

We allow triumph to become tragedy when we cover our ears to His love song, refusing to allow our bride-like hearts to be wooed and won, preferring to sit miserably on the cold concrete behind bars of steel instead of dancing with Him under His banner of love—all while the jail door stands open, offering freedom.

---

12. Ephesians 2:13
13. 1 Corinthians 6:19-20

Surely there is a hopeless romantic in the heart of every girl, that earnest craving for the perfect ending. And here, here is our chance to be freed from every former destruction and the heavy chains that have kept us from pursuing anything else. This is our opportunity to be crowned with lovingkindness and tender mercies.[14] So why wouldn't we run into His arms with His blood upon the doorposts of our hearts, and rejoice with every step towards the Promise Land of freedom?

I truly believe it's because we don't know the power of His Light.[15]

We've become so used to the power of darkness that has entrapped us, that we're unsure of how to respond to this tremendous shift, the conveying into the Kingdom of love, redemption, and forgiveness in Yeshua.[16] It's like we've been given a gift, but we're so overwhelmed by receiving it that we never tear away the pretty paper in order to see what's inside.

We receive Yeshua, but we don't unwrap the power His forgiveness holds.

You have been freely justified in grace and redemption,[17] and, as such, you have no condemnation in Messiah Yeshua as you walk in His Spirit.[18] The chains are off your wrists, sin has no hold on you, the door stands open. No, not because of your works, or your words, or your attempts at righteousness on your own, but only in His mercy has He washed you clean, renewing you with the Holy Spirit.[19] As far as the east is from the west, He has forgiven in His mercy.[20]

---

14. Psalm 103:4
15. John 3:18-21
16. Colossians 1:13-14
17. Romans 3:24
18. Romans 8:1
19. Titus 3:5
20. Psalm 103:8-12

You have been redeemed by His blood, forgiven by the riches of grace.[21]

This wasn't some afterthought or last-minute attempt to redeem you from a helpless state. This was a deliberate sacrifice, a giving of all so you can be made righteous by Yeshua who bore sin for you, giving you a pathway to become a beacon of Adonai's righteousness.[22] All your shortcomings, all the places where you feel like you just can't measure up—they're met with all you need in Messiah Yeshua. He will become the wisdom you seek, the righteousness you long for, the holiness that you feel is so out of your grasp, the redemption you never before thought could be possible.[23]

What more could you ask for of a glorious "Happily Ever After"?

With chains of shame and guilt fallen from your wrists, you are reconciled to Elohim and have been commissioned to go forth as a minister of reconciliation.[24] Such a powerful display of forgiveness and grace should drive us to an equivalent exhibition of love and mercy towards our fellow man.[25] Adonai cares about unity so passionately that He asks us to withhold our gifts of worship, and first go make amends with each other.[26]

No matter how uncomfortable it might feel, we can't shy away from our duty to reach out to those who have offended us and to those we have offended.

21. Ephesians 1:7
22. 2 Corinthians 5:21
23. 1 Corinthians 1:30
24. 2 Corinthians 5:18-19
25. Luke 7:47
26. Matthew 5:23-24

In order for us to resist being trapped by the shackles that once bound us, we must get rid of them once and for all by seeking forgiveness from others out of the forgiveness we've been given in Yeshua. Believe me, I understand how humbling a situation like this can be. I know other people aren't as willing to extend the forgiveness that Yeshua so readily offers.

Asking for forgiveness from others revives any dead consciouce your soul could possibly hide behind.

There have been many times in my life where I've had to ask for others' forgiveness, not because I wanted to, but because I know that is what Yeshua requires of me. The spirit is willing, the flesh is weak[27]—yet Yeshua is your strength.[28]

Leave all the darkness and baggage in the past, and enter into life abundantly in the forgiveness and light set before you.

When you've entered into covenant with Yeshua, there's no turning back:

Your heart has found all it has been searching for.

27. Matthew 26:41
28. 2 Corinthians 12:1

1.   Look up each verse footnoted in this chapter. Write the
       ones that spoke to your heart below.

2.   This chapter is so crucial to the rest of the book. In order
       to walk out your identity in Yeshua, you must first belong
       to Him. This is salvation! Like our forefathers in Egypt,
       have you placed Yeshua's blood upon the doorposts of
       your heart? What does that mean to you? What revealed
       your need for His salvation? If you have not, what is
       holding you back?

3. In what ways do you need Yeshua's covering to continue to seep in, transforming and removing the sin in your life where it starts (your heart)? This is sanctification.

4. What is one struggle in particular from which you need freedom? Perhaps it's guilt over something you've done, or a continual struggle with lust. How will you make real choices to walk in freedom through the power of Yeshua?

5. We all have broken parts of our lives, and stories that are sharp and sometimes hurt. Are you willing to trust Yeshua to make a beautiful mosaic out of those sharp pieces in your life?

6. How do you already see Yeshua rearranging broken pieces in your life to reveal a beautiful masterpiece for your good and for His glory?

7. Create a mosaic as a reminder of Yeshua's faithfulness and love to restore the things that are broken. You can make a traditional mosaic with broken pieces of glass and pottery, or make a mosaic out of paper by tearing up photos/ magazines/art and gluing the pieces on a canvas. As you're creating your masterpiece, be praying for Adonai to open your eyes to see the beautiful mosaic He is arranging in your life. Journal your revelations below!

8. In what ways have you allowed your sin to define you in the past? List the sins to which you have felt chained to.

9. Going back over the list you just wrote, cross out the sins you have allowed yourself to be defined by. Above each one you listed, write what defines you instead in Yeshua (i.e. freedom   joy   )

    ~~guilt~~   ~~depression~~

10. In what ways have you allowed yourself to be the dragon
    that keeps you chained to your jail cell instead of walking
    in forgiveness? How will you embrace the "Happily Ever
    After" Yeshua offers you?

11. What does the word "freedom" mean to you? What
    emotions does it stir in your soul, and how do you want
    to live in it?

12. Spend some time in prayer, and ask Adonai to reveal anyone from whom you need to ask forgiveness. Ask Him to forgive you, and then write a note of apology to this person to ask for their forgiveness. Pray over the words you need to speak, and write from a sincere and humble heart. Be sure to mail it or give it to them in person.

CHAPTER TWO

You Are Beautiful

Dear Beautiful You,

It's so true- there could never be a more beautiful you.

Don't shake your head or roll your eyes, trying to shimmy into the lies. In a world that flaunts its stuff, I know it's hard to believe that you're beautiful compared to the airbrushed model on the magazine cover at the checkout stand. I know it's hard to believe you're beautiful standing next to that person who is a size or two, or maybe even eight, smaller than you. I know it's hard to believe you're beautiful when you're caught on a bad hair day with looming deadlines and feel like you don't have enough of yourself to go around.

But here's the thing—you are beautiful. It's the hard truth, and a hard choice to believe.

They say the truth hurts, but really it just hurts our self-centered core. We push away the truth in order to shield our own ideas and coddle our self-pitying demise. Believe me, I've shoved the truth into the corner for far too many years. I've had my fair share of tears, thinking the world will end because the acne won't go away, or because friends have shattered my world with their careless words and actions, or when I've compared myself to girls who are prettier and smarter and skinnier than I am until I could never measure up.

Comparison will rob you blind. It's a joy stealer.

You are YOU. Beautiful, unique, amazingly wonderful YOU. You're the size you are, the skin color you are, with hair the length and thickness and texture it is, all because Elohim crafted you that way...because it gave Him pleasure.[1] Every part of you, from the crown of your head to the soles of your feet, was crafted specifically and purposefully to give glory and honor to your Creator.[2]

The Creator of the constellations and mountain peaks and royal lions took the time to hand craft YOU.

Don't mar the beauty He's given you, beautiful girl, just because the world says you need to be different. Don't compare, because there is nothing and no one to compare yourself to. There's no one in the whole world who could come close to who you are–because Elohim created only one of you. Take it from me: starving yourself to fit into someone else's size, dressing to appease fashions and trends, cutting your hair and coloring it to look like someone on the screen will never bring you happiness or the confidence you seek.

Never. Ever, ever.

Looking outside of yourself, you will never see who Adonai has created you to be, and that is where happiness and confidence is found—in Him. In who He created you to be. To live fully alive in His promises, in His words of love and adoration spoken over your soul.

He dances over you.

You're not a mistake, beautiful girl. Your quirks and personality are given as gifts—temperaments, family history,

---

1.   1 Corinthians 12:18
2.   Psalm 139:14

and all. Yes, it will take years for you to grow into them and be confident in all Adonai has given you. I still don't have it down myself, and that's okay. But you know what? We can grow together to reach the highest heights when we embrace these giftings and let Elohim have His perfect way in our messy, broken lives.

You were hand knit by the Almighty.[3]

They say sticks and stones will break your bones and words will never hurt you. But the truth is that words will always hurt, deeply. I remember being thirteen, going to Torah study so self-conscious about the first three pimples I'd ever had. I remember *exactly* how many, *exactly* where they were in the corner of my forehead, because I also remember *exactly* the incredulous blunt words of "Do you have acne?" coming from a boy who was taller than I. I thought I would never be so humiliated again in my life...but I was wrong. Words kept coming, even from people I cared about, about my face, my birthmarks, my hair, the color of my feet, or the way I hold a pencil. My best friend made off-hand comments about the size of my body in a moment of jest, and to be honest, I still have to war hard against that lie, even all these years later. But this fact remains in the midst of critics and criticism of things we can't change:

If I believe Adonai is perfect, and that He does everything perfectly, then I have to believe He created me perfectly, too.[4]

During that season when others' words burned and seared so deep into my soul, I had to take a look again at who Adonai said I am, and I hope you take a look, too. Perhaps you're at this same place where I was—desperate for truth, desperate to hear words of beauty. In a place where I felt so

3.   Psalm 139:15
4.   Deuteronomy 32:4

unloveable, I had to arm myself to battle against the lies that tried to make me doubt His goodness and His sovereignty. I had to sharpen my arrows with the truth that He truly does all things for our good.

He makes everything beautiful in His time.[5]

Even in your moments when you don't feel your loveliness, dear beautiful you, it's never far away. Beneath the surface of your skin, your soul perceives that Adonai still reigns on high and that you are engulfed in Yeshua's banner of love.[6]

It is this same banner which says there is no flaw in you, His beloved.[7]

There are many days when I still have to battle against the lies and distractions, to shoot down the accusations of the enemy which cause me to take my eyes off of the Kingdom and onto my flesh. It's a battle that, as women, we are never finished fighting. We all desire beauty, and even from the beginning, we've fallen prey to the lies and deceptions of what the world tells us beauty should be. When Eve took hold of the beautiful fruit in the Garden of Eden, it didn't live up to all her expectations, and sin and darkness stole from her the beautiful life she lived in the midst of an earthly paradise. But let me tell you a little secret, a secret that, had Eve taken hold of it, would have changed the entire course of history. It's a no-fail plan that defeats self-pity and comparison in its tracks:

The enemy cannot stand in the presence of gratitude.

Had Eve chosen gratitude over coveting more than what she was given, this world would have been an entirely different

---

5.   Ecclesiastes 3:11
6.   Song of Songs 2:4
7.   Song of Songs 4:7

place. Standing here, we can see the changed trajectory gratitude would have had. But I challenge you, gratitude in your own life can have just as big of an impact, even generational.

Like mother, like daughter.

How you view yourself as a masterpiece of Adonai will influence the way your daughters view themselves as well. Choosing gratitude now is laying a sure foundation for all those coming behind you, and even all those younger girls who are watching you today. When you feel like complaining, battle it with praise. You may not have size 0 hips or thighs, but you have legs that work and take you where you need to go. You may not be your idea of a perfect weight, but you're healthy and strong. You may not have a face clear from acne, but you have the opportunity to shine Yeshua's love through your eyes.

You may not look like Miss Universe, but the Maker of the Universe celebrates you.

Maybe you don't have legs that work. Maybe you're sick and weak, maybe you're unable to help yourself in the way you would like. Maybe you've been scarred from horrible chapters you never wished to have in your story, and you feel like your soul is marred from any beauty Adonai could ever see.

Elohim still sings over you.[8]

Your body—no matter the shape, size, color, experiences, or performance—is more than just a shell that holds your soul. You're not here to just exist amongst creation void of purpose and destiny. You're not here to be a walking masquerade for people to admire external artistry without seeing the real and raw you. No, you are so much more—your body is fashioned

---

8.   Zephaniah 3:17

after a palace,[9] a temple to host the living Elohim,[10] a cup to overflow with the weight of His glory. Your body is more than just a place in which your being dwells—it's chosen to be the dwelling place of the *Melech*[11] of the Universe.[12]

You're not your own, and how you honor your body is a glimpse in the mirror of how you honor Adonai.[13]

Truly, the most beautiful people I know are the ones who embrace all God has created them to be. They know that worldly beauty is only skin deep. Instead, they cultivate His kind of beauty in their hearts and lives, and it shines so brilliantly to those around them. Life is more than having the cutest outfit, or looking the most put-together. Rather than seeking the latest fashion trends which are here today and gone next season, Adonai is wanting to call out within us the things that are precious to Him—traits like patience, gentleness, and humility.[14]

Not only did He create you beautifully, His opinions of a beautiful soul accentuate all your natural beauty as you develop beautiful character.

Our character is so important, because it testifies to our relationship with Adonai. In 1 Peter 3, we're shown the matriarch Sarah as an example of what to pattern our desire for beauty after. This passage lists character traits and how Sarah submitted herself to Abraham, her husband. It's an impressive description, but she's not the only Biblical woman known for being beautiful, body and soul. To be fair, not all the beautiful women in Scripture shone forth Elohim's glory as they allowed their power, pride and trust in their appearances to be their downfall. Nevertheless, one beautiful woman who is

9.   Psalm 144:12
10.   1 Corinthians 6:19-20
11.   "King" in Hebrew
12.   1 Corinthians 3:16
13.   1 Corinthians 3:17
14.   1 Peter 3:3-6

often overlooked in her quiet humility is Abigail, wife of King David. Her short story in 1 Samuel 25 could easily be brushed under the history books, outshone by so many other women of valor with stories much longer than hers. Yet, as you dig deeper into this beautiful woman's life, you notice that although she is introduced as a beautiful woman,[15] it's the depth of her character that shines the brightest. David is not taken by her outward appearance—although she was stunning—and instead he is enraptured by her desire to have Adonai honored in his life, as well as her own.[16] Considering that David was, at the time, the most notorious outcast in all the country, I'm certain she had heard the stories and rumors of his escapades. Yet, she still put herself on the line in order to help him live in a way that pleased Adonai.

Clearly, beauty is not perfection of flesh, but perfecting the soul.

When I think of modern-day beautiful women who put the perfecting of their souls over the perfection of their bodies, my friend Sierra[17] comes to mind. Sierra is blind, but blindness doesn't define Sierra. I smile just thinking of her, because Yeshua's love radiates from every aspect of her. She can't see the beauty around her, so she creates it. Her smile never leaves her face and it literally lights up an entire room, causing you to smile right along with her. Sierra makes every person feel loved with hugs that feel like you've come home in a way unlike anything I've ever experienced before. She doesn't let blindness slow her down or prevent her from doing hard things and taking hold of all Adonai has for her. Sierra stands out from a crowd in a glorious way, because she embraces every ounce of beauty Elohim has showered over her. She knows her worth, the price that was paid out of His overwhelming love for her.

---

15.   1 Samuel 25:3
16.   1 Samuel 25:23-35
17.   Name changed

I don't know about you, but I'd take Sierra's beautifully full life over that of an eternally-empty fashion model's.

Sierra is not the only one. Another dear friend, Katelyn, comes to mind. Katelyn lost some vision in her left eye in an explosive accident several years ago, but she doesn't allow herself to spend her life always looking backwards at what could have been different. Instead, she digs deeper into what Yeshua sings over her so that she is unshakably rooted in her identity in Him. She truly is one of the most beautiful women I know, someone I'm constantly challenged and inspired by. She rejects all lies of the enemy and goes forth boldly in worship and praise for all the blessings in her life. Her laughter is so contagious, showering joy wherever she goes. Her prayers shake the courts of Heaven. When you worship next to Katelyn, you experience a wave of what it will be like when Yeshua's Kingdom comes. Katelyn knows exactly who she is to Yeshua, and as a result, she boldly lives in truth. She doesn't compare herself to others because she knows that there isn't anyone else to compare herself to.

She knows she is beautiful, and I hope you know that, too.

Oh yes, I hope you know what a gem you are, how you were created with all your many facets to reflect all the characteristics of Adonai. I hope you combat every deception and lie of the enemy, and turn it on its head with an out loud "Thank You" for the body He has crafted. I hope, too, that you'll do what I do every time I come far too close to not liking the image I see in the mirror—I hope you look yourself square in the eye and shout it out:

"I WILL PRAISE You for I AM fearfully and WONDERFULLY made." [18]

---

18.   Psalm 139:14

It's a declaration. I *will praise* Adonai today, and every day, for I *certainly* am fearfully and *wonderfully* made. It's concrete truth, concrete security, and a shield around us when the enemy and loose-lipped friends spill their negativity. It's a battle cry of victory, the song of a beautiful girl redeemed from deception and baggage.

Oh yes, beautiful you, there could be no other more beautiful creation of you.

Yet even with all this truth, I know you are still probably uncertain behind tattered curtains of doubt. As much as I wish I could, I can't make you believe it in the depths of your heart. I can't pry open your eyes to see what a wonderful creation you are, hand sculpted with so much love. Those are conscious choices you have to make yourself, standing on your own two feet in His confidence. And as you do, I pray you will reject the voices of the enemy and fully embrace with gratitude the amazingly beautiful woman you are. I pray you will rejoice in all of God's goodness towards you, flowing forth freely in engulfing waves. I pray you will delight—with every fiber of your being—in every good gift He has given you.[19] I pray that you own in your soul everything He has created you to be: beautiful, perfect, complete.

Breathe in His declarations. Exhale your grateful praise.

---

19. James 1:17

1.   Look up each verse footnoted in this chapter. Write the
       ones that spoke to your heart below.

2.   How can you be intentional in making the choice to
       believe Elohim's truth over the enemy's lies?

3.   Do you believe that Adonai is perfect, that He creates
       everything perfectly in His wisdom, and as a result has
       created you perfectly for His glory? Write your answer in
       big bold letters as a testimony and reminder to your soul!

4. List some things about your body that are hard for you to accept as beautiful.

5. Now, list truths/gratitudes to combat each lie and negative thought you wrote above.

6. With a permanent marker, blot out every deceptive item you listed in the first exercise. As you cross out each word, pray and ask Adonai to blot out these lies you've been believing in your heart as well. Write your prayer below.

7. With a highlighter, color every truth you listed. As you highlight each word, pray and ask Adonai to help you develop this kind of grateful mindset towards the body He has so beautifully created. Share any revelations below.

8. What do you think of when you picture a temple? How would this image change the way you view your body?

9. What are some beautiful character traits you want to develop in your life?

10. What kind of generational legacy do you want to leave to your daughters and granddaughters?

11. Do you have someone like Sierra or Katelyn in your life, someone who shines the beauty of Yeshua wherever they go? Name some women like these who inspire you towards true beauty.

12. On a sticky note, write out Psalm 139:14 and paste it on your bathroom mirror. Each day as you get ready (or every time you feel tempted to think negative thoughts about your appearance) shout this verse out loud with a heart of thankful praise!

CHAPTER THREE

You Are Chosen

Dear Chosen You,

Sometimes it feels like you're the only one still sitting on the sidelines, but let me tell you:

You are chosen by Adonai for greatness.

Yes, chosen for greatness. I know, sometimes it's a hard thing for me to believe too, when I watch everyone else around me score big on the field of life—big adventures, marriage, babies, college degrees, paparazzi moments. Everyone else seems to be going strong, while many days I feel like I'm barely treading water.

You understand too, don't you?

In fact, that's how this book came to be, born out of a season of lackluster unknown. The summer I was twenty-two was a hard and lonely season. I was single at family weddings, watching my friends enter into motherhood, standing nearby while girls I've mentored entered college and charted courses for their lives.

Left behind while others had grand adventures.

That summer, my only plan was to return to Israel, my soul's true home. My heart quickened to be in the Land again, and I had a sparkle in my eye when people asked me when I would be going. I had a goal to be Home again- to *daven*[1] at the *Kotel*[2], to taste the goodness of the Land, to cry at Shiloh. My heart beat with wild passion—for the Land, for the people, for relentless prayer—for something important to do.

That is, until it all abruptly unraveled and I was left with an entirely open autumn before me, while my peers continued on their great expeditions without me.

It was heartbreaking. I felt left out, overlooked. Like life was flying past me, and here I was, still sitting on the bench at the edge of the field while others scored big on the leaderboard. Or, more literally, I was left sitting on the swing of my back porch.

How we value our task determines how we respond with joy.

Instead of crying over it (or rather, after I already had) I took this silence as a gift and an opportunity. Every night over that summer, I took to that creaking porch swing with prayer, my laptop, and a cold treat to beat the sticky humidity. Through mosquito bites and perspiration, I prayed over the words that flowed from my fingers. I prayed for Adonai to speak through me, and most importantly—I prayed over you, reading this now, wherever you are in the world.

Sometimes our greatest heartbreak is the launching pad for our greatest success.

The School of Hard Knocks is never fun, never something we enjoy. But instead of bemoaning our hardships, what if we chose to do something about it? What if we chose purpose—

---

1. Traditionally, praying Jewish liturgical prayers with a back and forth swaying motion.
2. The Western Wall

and even joy—while we're in it, while we're struggling through the trenches? What if we saw disappointments as our greatest opportunities, straight from Adonai's heart to ours?

No matter your situation, you are chosen for such a time as this.[3]

I don't know what your circumstances are, or how you may feel left behind. Maybe you didn't get picked for a part in the play, maybe your application for an expedition got denied. Maybe you failed your grade, or feel like you're the only girl without an important career path ahead of you. Maybe you feel like you'll be single the rest of your life—or maybe you are married, but you feel like you'll be wading in the trenches of motherhood forever.

Whatever the case- you were ordained to be here by Adonai Tzvaot.

You are here, and it's not because Adonai is withholding something better from you down the road. It's not because He wants to inflict disappointment to your heart or scribble out your dreams. No, you are here because this is the best place for Him to bless you—to shower you with His good gifts from above. You're here because you are most effective for His Kingdom at this place and season in time. You're here because He has great plans for you—not just for tomorrow, but for TODAY[4].

You are here for abundant life and blessing, even in your mundane tasks of everyday.[5]

The greatest hero is one who serves unnoticed and unthanked. The one who sweeps the kitchen and scrubs the

---

3.   Esther 4:14
4.   Jeremiah 29:11
5.   Romans 5:17

toilets and wipes the spit-up off another woman's child. The one who is silently faithful to His still small voice, ears straining to hear His directions in the wind. The one who is plodding on through the trenches of real life, waiting for confirmation to move beyond to a more spacious plain.

Before she was Queen, Esther was right in your boat.

The older I get, the more the story of Esther inspires me. It's not just a princess fairy tale, one where the pauper is picked and escorted into riches. No, I see a girl just like you and me. She swept floors and served her cousin Mordecai; she made meals and wondered what her purpose was in it all. She lived in the rabble, she worked and performed the mundane tasks of life.

Her kingdom life didn't come overnight, but every faithful sweep of her broom brought her one moment closer.

Throughout her entire story, Esther's character remains the same. Obedient. Trusting. Loving. Sacrificing. Providing encouragement and nourishment to those around her. Against her free choice, she's married to a man who wants to kill her people, yet she woos his heart with her grace, and he loves her for it. Contrary to the glamorous life we imagine it to be as we read the pages of her scroll, it wasn't greatness that was thrust upon her. Esther didn't seek it out, she didn't run to find it. Other dreams died when she was brought to the palace. Being queen wasn't her goal, or something she had to strive for.

She was simply born for this, and nothing stands in the way of the purpose God has created for us.[6]

Esther was proven faithful in her performance of the ordinary. She took regular steps of faith and they led her to the King's table. She did it all with such beautiful courage, even

---

6.   Psalm 57:2

when her heart quaked within her. Adonai knew He could trust her to intercede on behalf of His people because He had seen her steady faithfulness every moment of the poor life she lived in her cousin's home.[7] She didn't complain, didn't murmur.[8]

She listened for His voice and obeyed in the tasks He set before her, no matter how big or small.

I don't know about you, but I want to be an Esther. I'm not holding my breath for the world's most powerful ruler to fall in love with me over my beauty—I'm not taking her story that literally—but I want to live boldly in the place Adonai has me. Reading the pages of the book of Esther, it reminds me and confirms in my heart that the thing that I was born to do will come about, and nothing will stop it. Every faithful step I take, the Kingdom is one step closer.

We live with the Kingdom on the horizon, with the heart of a queen within.

Yes, if we have the heart of a queen within, we're already on our way to understanding our place in the seasons we're in. We start to answer the question, "What must I do?" by asking instead, "Who must I be?" We look internally to see if we have the character to endure each circumstance with grace, with perseverance, with steadfast love in Adonai, instead of frantically trying to find our place and social status.[9] It's not about the part we weren't chosen for, or the grade we didn't get, or whether or not there's a ring on our finger.

---

7.   Matthew 25:21
8.   Philippians 2:14-16
9.   James 1:2-4

Rather, it's who we become through it all.

It's becoming confident in who Adonai has created you to be, how He's chosen you specifically for the tasks He has set in your midst. You are not misplaced, and not overlooked. You're not sitting on the outskirts of the field for nothing.

You're here for a reason.

Recall your strengths and how you can apply them here and now, right where you are, right where it seems so impossible for them to shine. This is your moment, even here on the bench. Maybe you're a servant, picking up the extra tasks of those playing hard on the field. Maybe you're a nurturer, taking care of those who hobble off injured. Maybe you're a leader, showing everyone else sitting on the bench how it looks to wait on Adonai. Or maybe you're an encourager like me, trying to keep up the morale of everyone playing in the game.

If Adonai is asking me to sit on the bench in this season, rather than chasing all my big dreams, then I'm going to sit here and shout encouragement at the top of my voice.

We were chosen to praise Him, no matter the circumstances, confident of our identity in Yeshua. He calls you royal, holy, and special, from the depths of His heart. He is as much invested in your life, no matter how small and quiet it may seem, as He is invested in all the people you know who are out there in the thick of doing great things.

There is no comparison with Elohim.

In the same way He has chosen you, He asks us to choose each other.[10] Before the foundation of the world, He chose you

---

10. Romans 15:7

to be holy and blameless in love.[11] He wants us to choose others the way that He chose us, by seeing their potential, by fanning their calling into a passionate flame without comparing them with others or yourself. Their tasks and giftings may be so different from yours, but it doesn't mean either are less special side by side.

We are chosen to work better together.

It's not about your part or their part. It's about working *b'yachad*, together. Wherever you are, be all in, fully invested to the cause of the Kingdom. Take a step back and see the Kingdom playing field as it really is, not just a stage for performance. It doesn't matter if it's not how you envisioned your life would be. When does anything come out the way we craft our glitzy dreams to be? Embrace the muddy fields, embrace this time to shine forth, chosen by Adonai in this place—and yes, even embrace the thrills of adventure others are experiencing in the midst of the game.

You are chosen for such a time as this.

---

11. Ephesians 1:4

1.   Look up each verse footnoted in this chapter. Write the
       ones that spoke to your heart below.

2.   Have you experienced a situation recently where you felt
       left out or overlooked?

3.   In the above situation, how did an attitude of self pity
       influence your outlook?

4. In the same way, how would an attitude of opportunity have influenced your outlook, and what would it have caused you to do instead?

5. Elohim works all things for our good, including what we view as hard or painful or unfair. What is a hard/painful/ unfair situation you experienced where after you walked through this trial, you realized Adonai was working it all for your good? What was the lesson you learned through it?

6. List some ways you are most available and effective for the Kingdom in this season you're in.

7. Think of a silent hero who goes unnoticed and unthanked in your own life. What could you learn from this person's faithfulness? This week, what way could you show this person gratitude for all they do?

8. How does Esther's story speak to your own heart?

9.   What are some little things you can be faithful in this week?

10.   Answer this question, based on Scripture: "Who must I be?"

11.   It's hard to be happy for others when they receive something we've always wanted. How can you choose to love others in this situation, and how can you use your strengths and talents for their encouragement and benefit?

CHAPTER FOUR

You Are Not Alone

Dear Social You,

You are not alone.

I know there are days it feels like you are. The highway of holiness is not a popular one, and very few walk the tightrope of Torah anchored by Yeshua's sacrifice. Standing trembling on that highwire, watching others jump ship, it's hard to keep taking those steps forward into what seems like excommunication from civilization. I get the feelings of isolation, of loneliness, the feeling like you're taking Elijah's place, saying you're the last righteous one left on planet earth.

Yet here's the truth: Adonai has still reserved His 7,000.[1]

He doesn't say what this 7,000 looks like or who they are, but based on my past experiences, if I were to make an educated guess, I'd say they're not all peers your age. They probably don't live next to you either, otherwise you wouldn't be feeling this aching for companionship in your soul.

Our definition of friendship has to be blown out of the water.

Most of my life, I didn't have a close community of friends my age. My family was always growing and seeking, attending

---

1.   Romans 11:2-5

many different congregations, often just a few weeks after I felt like I was finally settling in. In the midst of it, it was so difficult, so emotionally draining, feeling like I would never have a place to belong. I had friends across the country, even across the world who I kept up with via letters and texts, but let's admit: it's not the same as catching up over coffee or going on a thrift store expedition together.

In the middle of it was hard, but today, I'm crazy grateful.

Not having nearby friends my age forced me to see beyond my generation, season, and situation to the rest of the community outside my preconceived notions. For example, I have a beautiful friend named Jennifer, who is a wife, mother, and years my senior. I met her one Shabbat at a new congregation, and I'll be honest, that day I came pretty close to closing my eyes to the rest of the Body of Messiah by allowing myself to wallow in self-pity that there was no one my age there. Had I done that, I would have totally missed Jennifer's bubbly personality and how we connected instantly with our passionate pursuit of the Kingdom, with the ability to dissolve laughing over our mistakes until our stomachs hurt.

Souls have no age gap, because life is a love story—all of us seeking to be loved and noticed.[2]

When I take my eyes off of *me*, I see *them*. I see elderly widows who are overwhelmed with delight to share an awkward tea with me—because when you live alone, you embrace awkward company. I see young mothers so grateful for an out-of-the-blue delivery of homemade cookies and iced coffees. I see grandpas with war stories to tell, and as I ask them questions they regain their dignity and sense of worth. I

---

2.   Romans 12:10

see little girls whose eyes shine so bright when I pay attention to them—to make them feel important, to know that someone twice their age thinks of them as a special friend.

You may not have friends your age, but you have an entire community who desperately needs you.[3]

Don't let the fear of awkward and unknown keep you from reaching out. Cry out in prayer to be given the eyes of Yeshua, to see others as He saw them when He walked this earth. Have eyes of compassion, not comparison, and remember—it's not about you. Keep fighting back the feelings of discouragement and despair.[4]

You are a world-changer. A community-builder.

When I think of a woman who is actively pursuing a bigger community, my sweet friend Marili comes to mind. We met in the vineyards of Israel, but live oceans apart—she is in South Africa, I am in the States. Recently, Marili felt like the Father was asking her to relocate to be closer to her parents, which required her to leave her tight-knit group of friends and strong community. She kept marching boldly forward in the Father's will, even though it felt lonely and unfamiliar. At times she felt scared and out of her comfort zone. In an effort to connect with others, she made it a priority for herself to attend different congregations and social events where she knew hardly anyone. She still doesn't have that tight-knit feel of community like the one she left behind, but it doesn't stop her from reaching out and trying. She calls up the people she does know to grab coffee together and she's intentional in investing in the lives of her friends around the globe.

---

3. 1 Corinthians 12:25-27
4. Deuteronomy 31:8

*Marili seeks to build a better community by following
Adonai's voice, trusting that He is going to lead her to the
people who need her most.*

But even for Marili, it can get exhausting always reaching
out and giving to others without feeling like your soul is
replenished. I know how tiring it gets sometimes, how you
feel like you're always giving and giving but never receiving.
Sometimes it feels like you're broken—broken like *challah*,[5]
then passed around until you feel like there is no crumb left for
yourself. And slowly...you begin to feel resentment.

That's a place we should never want to be.

If we're at that place, we turn bitter—self-focused instead
of others-focused. So consumed with our own comfort, that
we withhold that last morsel of nutrition for ourselves rather
than giving it to another soul in desperate need. Here's the
deal: We're not asked to give only to those who appreciate
it. We're not asked to invest only in friendships that are easy
with people we know. We're not asked to reach out only if they
have certain personalities. No, this covers the socialites and
wallflowers alike:

We're asked to give all, to all, as He has given to us.[6]

Loneliness is a deception that drains you dry, shriveling
your soul and clenching your fist to the world around you. It
steals our sight and blinds our eyes to see this whole wide world
filled with all these souls looking for hope and love. When we
choose to see, when we live with hands cracked open to grace,
we will be broken and poured out. But, more than that, we will
be blessed sevenfold.

---

5.   Traditional Jewish braided bread, used in celebrating the beginning of
      the Sabbath
6.   Deuteronomy 16:17

Whatever we do to the least of these, we do to the King.[7]

Being broken like challah, passed around, it may not be something we would choose to do if we were here to protect our flesh from pain and hurt. Yet, isn't this what Yeshua has done for us?[8] Yes, and we will do it—whatever reaching out or giving we're asked to do—in remembrance of Him. There's no place you walk, no emotion you're feeling that He hasn't felt or experienced too.[9] He's cheering you on, reminding you of His Father's words:

I am with you.[10]

Yes, you. The Creator of the galaxies commits to walking right next to you, bending low to take your hand. No paparazzi or friends could ever measure up to the glory of this, no amount of cliques or bosom friends could ever touch the depth of this kind of devoted love.

Through fire and flood, His presence is fast and sure.[11]

I don't know about you, but in my life His presence is the only anchor I can count on. Communities shift, people fly in and out, changing and circling with moves, new seasons, jobs, different paths and different beliefs, *but not Adonai.* Adonai is the only One I know I can always call, and He'll be there to answer me.[12] Steady and secure. He is life and joy, a deep well with a wealth of wisdom that will never run dry.

---

7.   Matthew 25:40
8.   Matthew 26:26
9.   Hebrews 4:15
10. Isaiah 41:10
11. Isaiah 43:2
12. Jeremiah 33:3

He is the only one who can fill back up my dry and empty cup.[13]

In all my giving and reaching out, if I'm not filling myself up with sweet communion with my heavenly Father, I am only giving of my flesh and of myself—doing more harm than good, especially to myself. You, me, and Marili, have to remember that in order to give, we have to be filled. Filled with Scripture, filled with the Spirit, filled with the overwhelming love and goodness of Adonai's blessing in our lives.

In this season that feels secluding and dry, use it for drawing deeper into Yeshua's heart.

Have you ever thought that this may be the reason why you're at these crossroads? That it's a desperate plea from the Lover of your heart to be pursued the way He pursues you? How He longs to fill your life with such a deep richness of purpose and belonging, that will stay with you far longer than a casual coffee date with an acquaintance. His heart beats to reveal to you His Covenant of Love, written in His blood throughout the pages of Scripture.

Yes, there is a Friend who sticks closer than a brother.[14]

Your Heavenly Abba and your Yeshua stand near, both longing for an intimate friendship with you. There is no excuse for loneliness when all the love and support you could ever need is standing at the door, waiting to come into the garden of your heart.[15] Above all, this is my prayer for you: to take this season and dive deep into the waters of His love that cannot be quenched.[16] There's nothing I want more for you than to

---

13. Psalm 23:5
14. Proverbs 18:24
15. Song of Songs 4:16
16. Song of Songs 8:7

have you fall radically in love with Him. To know His likes and dislikes, to seek to bring Him joy and praise. To have Him be the fire in your veins, the pulse of passion in your life, illuminating and bringing warmth to whatever season you're in.[17]

To delight in His friendship over anything else in all creation.

Yes, this season isn't forever, and Adonai will continue to bring people in and out of your life. Some may be close friends your age, and others, a scattering of community rallying around you. Through rise and fall, as spring turns to summer and summer into autumn, you have this hope as an anchor for your soul:

Yeshua is there, and you are never alone.[18]

---

17. Hebrews 12:28-29
18. Hebrews 6:19-20

1. Look up each verse footnoted in this chapter. Write the
      ones that spoke to your heart below.

_____

_____

_____

_____

_____

_____

_____

_____

_____

_____

_____

2. Read Elijah's story in 1 Kings 19. Take note of how Adonai
      sent angels to minister to him in his despair, and how
      Elijah's time of solitude became a place of refreshment at
      the Mountain of Elohim. Adonai meets with Elijah in His
      gentleness and mercy, revealing that Elijah is not alone
      in his tasks. The chapter wraps up with Elisha joining
      Elijah in his ministry, a gift of physical companionship
      from Adonai. Write your thoughts from this chapter of
      Scripture below.

_____

_____

_____

_____

_____

_____

_____

_____

_____

3. Answer these personal questions drawn from Elijah's life as recorded in this chapter:

- How is Adonai ministering to my soul in this season?

- How can I quiet my soul to find refreshment at the Mountain of Elohim?

- What is Adonai speaking to me in His still small voice?

- Has Adonai given me a companion like Elisha who I haven't noticed before, and if not, how can I be intentional in praying for this kind of Kingdom-minded friend to come into my life?

4. Read through 1 Corinthians 12:6-31. How does this change your perspective on community? Why do we all need each other?

5. How can you be intentional in building community?

6. Talk with your parents or elders (or if married, your husband!) and do some research. Are there any upcoming events, local groups, or publications you could get connected with?

7. Maybe you don't have any community near you whatsoever. How can you change that? Is there a gathering or evening you could host to build community around you? How about inviting a friend for coffee?

8. Who are some women—older and younger—whom you could befriend?

9. Think of others in your life who are lonely, overlooked, or who may seem too busy with their lives to make time for others. What are some practical things you can do to invest in them?

10. On a scale of 0-5, rate yourself on how intentional you are in being fulfilled in Yeshua rather than in friends.

11. How can you be even more intentional to pursue Adonai's heart?

12. List some things you want to discover more deeply about Adonai (i.e. what He loves, what brings Him glory, etc.). Use this list as a springboard to search Scripture, discover the answers, and spend time in His presence!

CHAPTER FIVE

You Are Gifted

Dear Gifted You,

You have so much to offer.

You are amazingly creative, a vessel that holds incredible talents. Don't ever let shame keep you from creating, from sharing your gifts with the world, from presenting your offerings to others.

Don't let shame keep you from being happy with what your hands have made.

We live in a world that's overstimulated. There are images and goals and posters of what the perfect project must be. We live in a world that's curated and edited and glossy. We read blogs with perfect presentations. Projects on Pinterest that never seem to have the same results when we attempt them and Instagram where no one has a bad hair day.

It's a lot of pressure. A high bar, where looking up suffocates you from all joy and potential.

I should know. For years I was ashamed to call myself a writer. A seamstress. An artist. My work seemed so incomplete and imperfect compared to others who held a standard far above my reach. I allowed shame to keep me in the dark, chained to doodling and writing and creating in my room, away from others' eyes.

To hide your Adonai-given talents is to hide your light under a basket.[1]

The desires and abilities He has given to your soul were given for all the world to see. They were gifts made to shine for His glory, to come alongside the Creator in embellishing His already magnificent creation.

Your gifts are an invitation to co-create with the Creator, and there is nothing you do that doesn't delight His heart.

What you offer—the presents you bring forth from the depths of your soul—paint the attributes of Creator Elohim in magnificently spectacular ways. You were created in His image, and as such, your heart beats for this:[2] to show the world your strokes of color, to shape and create and craft beauty for others to enjoy.

You create beauty, for you are altogether beautiful.[3]
Worthy. Loved. Amazing.

Here's the truth: beauty is not always perfection, and imperfections can be beautiful. After all, Elohim delights to take broken things and broken people and make something so much better from the pieces. Life is about the journey of learning, growing, and being shaped into the person Adonai created you to be, with all your flaws included. Perfection ends the journey, so embrace those imperfect moments that you can learn from and create character within.

Let fear, perfectionism, and shame fall into the depths of the sea.

I get it, that it's a battle. Every artist—no matter who they are or how professional they may be at their craft—always sees

---

1.   Matthew 5:14-16
2.   Genesis 1:27
3.   Song of Songs 4:7

the flaws in their work. There are always highs and lows, times where it's easy to soar in all Adonai has created you to be, and times where you feel the shackles of comparison chafe around your wrists.

Yet this can't be our exception, because this is the rule: comparison is coveting, and it's breaking the 10th commandment.[4]

Written in tablets of stone, transferred to the tablet of your heart,[5] is an open invitation—no, a command—to let all the chains and shackles we inflict upon ourselves fall to the wayside. It's a freedom pass, freeing us to create and reach our fullest potential without causing ourselves to be crushed by that our of neighbor. If we kept this in mind, how would it change our craft, and how much more free would we feel?

Please, don't hide your talents any longer.

The truth is, no one can tell your story from your unique perspective like you can. You are beautifully you in every area. Don't let comparison lock the shackles of shame on your soul. Others do not outshine you with all you have to offer, and you don't have to run or apologize your way out of the spotlight. It doesn't matter how unskilled you feel or how small your talents may seem.

The biggest question is not their size, but what you will do with them.

The Parable of the Talents[6] is such a powerful story told by Yeshua, so applicable to this topic, and not just because of the word "talents" in its title. Like the servants in this tale, we each have been entrusted with a precious gift, its wonder weighing heavily in our hands like sparkling gold coins.

---

4.   Exodus 20:17
5.   Jeremiah 31:33
6.   Matthew 25:14-29

We each will be called to give an account at our Master's return, but which of the servants will we be? [7]

The servant who was given five talents was dedicated, investing the generous amount he already had in order to hone his talents to their utmost potential. The servant who was given two talents was grateful, developing the small amount he had in order to grow his talents bit by bit.

Yet, the servant who was given one talent failed in fear.

This servant had just as much opportunity to grow and improve and multiply his talents, but he let fear chain him down. I'm sure he was aware of his fellow servants who were busy with the talents they were given, yet instead of following their example, he did nothing at all. He had a wealth of potential locked inside, but instead of digging deep into his soul, he dug deep for its burial into the soil. [8]

His fear strangled the life he was meant to create.

You and I, do we do the same? Do we let fear strangle what we have to offer, holding us back like a cocoon of steel, trapping the butterfly within from ever unfurling its beautiful wings? Do we shove our talents deep into our pocket in shame, ignoring the way they're still pressing into our soul, acting like they don't exist? Do we feel guilty about our small giftings, brushing them off like they're nothing instead of seeing their incredible worth?

Our talents are gifts given to us, but they don't belong to us. [9]

We see our talents as something we own, something that's a part of who we are. However, the ownership doesn't belong

---

7.   Romans 14:12
8.   Matthew 25:25
9.   Matthew 25:14-15

to us. They are all Adonai's talents, given to us on loan for our lifespan. Our talents aren't our identity. Yeshua is. Our talents aren't our fulfillment. Yeshua is. Our talents aren't our purpose or passion or the reason we're here. Yeshua is.

Adonai has given us this gift to draw us closer to Himself.

Each of our own special giftings were handed to us in order to see where our heart is. He wants to see our gratefulness for the gifts we've been given, He wants to see our faithfulness to maximize the impact of the tools we have. He wants to see what we'll do with what we're given, He wants to see what our perspective will be through them.

Out of our little, He wants to bless us with greater. [10]

Matthew 25:21 then becomes the mantra not just for the craft room, but for the kitchen, the schoolroom, the piano keys and the studio. It weaves the pulse of purpose into it all. That every beat of the whisk, every essay you pen, every waltz your fingers play, all the creating you do, is for one thing, and one thing alone:

That no matter what we do, we do it for Adonai's glory. [11]

Everything becomes a symphony of praise, an elaborate feast, a stunning exhibition, all for the audience of One. Critics' claims, once deafening, are no longer audible in the midst of His gentle laugh and praise. Our expressions of creativity become a romance between His heart and ours, a secret code where every stroke of our brush and every stitch of our needle become a love letter from our heart to His.

---

10. Matthew 25:21
11. 1 Corinthians 10:31

Obedience may be the proof of love,[12] but creativity shows the emotion behind it.

Adonai sculpts the world each day and in every season as a visual reminder of His love and care. He brings forth tulips to bloom out of the earth in the spring, He sends the splashing waves upon the shore all summer long, He delicately paints each leaf in a vibrant array of color every autumn, He tucks the world into a snug blanket of crystal snow as the weather turns to winter. In every song sung by the birds, in every rainbow hanging in the sky, in every awesome display of lightning, in every gentle breeze is a whisper:

"I love you"[13]

Perhaps, if we truly believed we were created in Adonai's image, we'd be intentional to do the same. Perhaps we'd find even more delight in expressing our creativity and be more intentional in developing our talents if we paused for a moment to be in awe of what Adonai does each and every day.

Perhaps our talents would take on greater worth if we viewed them as an "I love you" back to the heart of Adonai.

No, dear gifted you, don't hide or hold back any longer. Share your story loud, paint it with all your favorite colors. Unlock your heart to share what it has to offer with boldness and grace. Decorate your world like only you can. Create a love song back to His heart with chords only you can play. Adonai has given you gifts, and they weren't by accident.

Use them fearlessly.

12.　1 John 5:2-3
13.　Isaiah 43:4

1. Look up each verse footnoted in this chapter. Write the ones that spoke to your heart below.

2. We all have talents, no matter how big or small. List some talents you believe you have.

3. Sometimes it's hard for us to see things in ourselves, while things within us are so evidently clear to others. Ask three people, a parent, teacher, sibling, grandparent, friend, or mentor, to share what talents they see in you. List their responses below.

4. In this chapter I shared how I used to be ashamed to call myself creative titles, such as an author and artist. What are some titles you've been ashamed to call yourself, and in what ways can you develop these areas to be the best YOU can be?

5. Think of an item you cherish that has imperfections but that you still view as beautiful. Perhaps it is a chipped teacup, an heirloom quilt, a faded recipe or a yellowed book. How do the imperfections of this item tell a story?

6. How do the imperfections of your life tell a story?

7. In what ways have you coveted the talents of others? Being specific, write out a prayer of repentance to Adonai below.

8. How does the Parable of the Talents motivate you to make changes in your life? In what ways can you be faithful in developing the talents Elohim has given you?

9. On a sticky note, write out Matthew 25:21 and paste it where it will be clearly visible wherever you do your creating. Anytime you are tempted to compare your work to others, or when you feel like hiding your talents in fear, speak this verse out loud, and then continue on, faithfully!

10. If you saw your creativity as a way to express the emotion of your love towards Adonai, how would it impact your dedication and intentionality in your creating?

11. What projects have always been on your heart, but you've been too afraid to start? How can you pursue them fearlessly?

12. Draw a heart next to Isaiah 43:4 in your Bible and underline Adonai's words to you: "I love you."

CHAPTER SIX

You Are Equipped

Dear Equipped You,

You don't have to be intimidated for this journey.

It's a little ironic that this was the chapter for which I had total writers' block. No matter how many times I opened this chapter, I stared at a blank screen and didn't know where to begin. Words just didn't seem to come fast and furious, so I was left to feel high and dry and without anything to offer.

I felt totally unequipped.

I was cheering on other friends in their wildly brave dreams, and yet I felt like mine were so out of reach. Like I didn't have the right things to offer. The enemy breathed down the back of my neck, sound waves visualizing in the pulse of the blinking curser on my blank screen, sending paralyzing shivers down my spine... "You don't have anything to offer. Not like your other friends. They have exciting things in store...but you? No. Not you."

A half truth mixed with a whole lie is just a big fat lie.

The enemy plays off of the emotions you already feel—the feelings of inadequacy, of intimidation and uncertainty to begin. Open the door a crack[1] and he'll weasel his way in,

---

1. Genesis 4:7

sliming every corner of your mind, baiting you on his hook with little half-truths and a then feeding you a whole lot of extra trash. I hate to say he's right, but his hook-line-and-sinker almost worked. He's correct in saying I don't have anything to offer like my other friends do. I could have grabbed the bait, but I knew the other half of the truth he failed to mention:

I only have what I have to offer.

No one can write from my perspective, or draw from the well the Father has given me. No one else can share my unique experiences, because I'm the only one who has walked through them in only the way I can. Every situation, every circumstance, everything Adonai has given me, it's all to equip me. It all forms a shield of strength around me, ready to battle on the fields where Elohim leads me. I can't let the enemy use words or thoughts, or even my friends to distract me from all my potential, simply because my potential doesn't look like that of the person standing next to me.

The enemy doesn't want you to just not finish your project. He doesn't even want you to begin it.

We have to stand on the truth that we are submitted to Adonai's authority and calling on our lives, and the devil will flee from before us.[2] There is no room in our minds or hearts for his schemes and sneaky language. You must be confident that every piece placed in your wildly beating heart—your heart longing for adventure and purpose and the pursuit of Adonai's plan for your life—are there in exact detail for all the glorious and amazing missions He has in store for you. In whatever shape or size you feel this calling, I know it's there. It'll be different from mine, different from your sister's, different from the girl you sit next to at services. We're not here to compare how shiny our armor is, or boast of the

2.   James 4:7

adventures we're having. We're all here for unique reasons, totally irreplaceable in our spheres of influence.

We all were created to go forth and shine, illuminating truth that cannot be hidden.[3]

For single women, it's easy to feel lost in this season of singleness, unsure of where we fit in or what our role is in this complex world of social statuses. For married women, it's easy to feel like your identity is wrapped in so many other things— your kids, your husband, the condition of your house—rather than who your soul is. We all look at the girl next to us in her passionate pursuits, and it leaves us feeling deflated instead of inspired. So many questions swirl in our minds that we don't even know where to begin. What does Adonai want us to do? How are we supposed to spend our time wisely? In what ways can we further His Kingdom, right here where we're at? The questions can become overwhelming, but I challenge you: if you stopped and took ten minutes to search for what sets your soul on fire, you'd never be more certain of anything in your life.

Our passions are given for His purposes.[4]

Tailored and handcrafted just for you, your passions and interests and hobbies are tools of the Kingdom when coupled with His vision. They're a means of transportation, of bringing Yeshua's presence into everything you touch. You were created for this, you are a piece of Adonai's workmanship to do good works through the name of Yeshua.[5]

You just have to identify them.

Perhaps you always played dress up as a child, or never tired of taking care of "sick" baby dolls. Maybe you were

3.   Matthew 5:14
4.   2 Timothy 1:9
5.   Ephesians 2:10

always rearranging the furniture in your dollhouse or couldn't stop doodling on anything you could get your pen on. Maybe creative stories always swirled in your head or you couldn't get enough of the outdoors. Certainly, there are many interests that come and go throughout your lifetime—I admit, I no longer spend much time dreaming of working at a zoo—but there are some that never change.

You've been given golden threads woven throughout the tapestry of your life, that have stood the test of time, and they direct you to the King's purposes.

For me, my golden threads are writing, creating, gathering Elohim's daughters together and encouraging them to pursue His holiness in their lives. It could take on so many different shapes and forms as these golden threads display themselves in textured embroidery, no two stitches alike. One day it may be writing this book—a huge undertaking for a big dreamer like myself—and another day it may be simply writing a note to a friend who is going through some hard times. One day it may be orchestrating a big event, while another day it may be making a birthday gift for a niece. Don't despise the small, and don't shrink back from the big.

When we hone our vision to focus on the things we know we do best, we become so much more effective for the Kingdom.

We can't allow ourselves to be distracted by our smaller interests in the pursuit of purposeful plans. For example, I may enjoy the art of photography, and even have an artistic eye for it, but it's not something I wake up each morning totally passionate about. Although I love coffee and may make a macchiato or two from time to time, I have very little skills otherwise, unlike my barista-skilled friend Kayla who can brew and steam just about any caffeine concoction. If I spent the majority of my time dabbling with my coffee skills (or lack thereof) or playing photographer, I would totally miss the point of *my* purpose. Purpose with my time, purpose with my skills.

Develop what you have, but take your best and make it shine.

In the same way, I can't allow myself to be distracted by other friends who have the same giftings as I do. I can't compare my work to the work that they do, or feel left out by their success. Those golden threads you've identified in your life sometimes become lifelines, grasping for truth to hang on to in the midst of a competing world. Sometimes you have to just close your eyes, breathe deep, and know:

I am shielded and kept in His glorious power until the end of time, decidedly qualified in Him.[6]

We can't allow ourselves to be intimidated by others on the battlefield, or by those who seem to have been given the perfect stage and spotlight while you've been given the back corner of the auditorium. We can't even allow ourselves to be overwhelmed with the possibilities of all the passions and pursuits we could take, eager to do something that will make the world a better place. Even after we've narrowed down our talents to one, two, or three things Adonai has equipped us in, we still may have a hard time walking boldly in them. It's not just the volume of our abilities that holds us back or hides that golden thread from view. There are so many more excuses we allow the enemy to tell us, and they distract us from being the best we can be. More half-truths-turned-full-lies, such as "We have no time." "No money." "Not enough talent, or not the right audience to receive our offerings.

---

6.   1 Peter 1:5

The truth is, you lack nothing.[7]

This is a verse that I have to speak over myself time and time again. I am fully equipped to pursue His callings on my heart, and I am fully supplied by His riches. How often, instead, do I want to shrink back and hide—hide in fear, hide in uncertainty, hide even in shame. Instead of fully embracing the story He has given me to tell, I want to crawl deep under my covers with my pillow over my head, terrified to tell it.

You and I can do all things through Yeshua who strengthens us.[8]

He doesn't promise our journey will be easy, but He does promise strength for the trials along the way. All the skills for your journey are right there, ready to be used. The spirit of wisdom has been poured upon you, coupled with the revelation of Yeshua to your heart, visualized with eyes of understanding.[9]

Girl, you are fully equipped, empowered by Adonai exactly for this time in His Story.

You are called and equipped to be an ambassador for Yeshua, shining in the avenues and places where He leads you.[10] As an ambassador, every part of you represents the King of Heaven, from the clothing you wear, to the words on your lips, and even the places you go. It all has a message, it all tells a story—either His, or yours.

It seems like a lot of pressure.

Imagine in your mind, being the ambassador to another country. Every person you come in contact with forms an

7.   Philippians 4:19
8.   Philippians 4:13
9.   Ephesians 1:17-18
10. 2 Corinthians 5:20

opinion of your country based on who you are. You must be professional and purposeful, on guard and driven. Don't let terror and fear take hold of you, because you are responsible for diplomacy and have a mission to accomplish.

This is your high calling.

This is another crossroad in pursuing that thing you're equipped for. No matter what you pursue, no matter what passions Elohim has given for you to use, every detail about you is a representation of *something*. You may be equipped, but what direction will you take with it? Is the message you're giving one of the world, or of the Kingdom? The world calls you to make a name for yourself, to do things big and loud and clamor on top of all your competitors. Yet, this was your calling before time began: you are saved by Him with lavish grace, called to a holy calling for His purposes. You are strengthened with all of Adonai's power, equipped for long-suffering with joy and patience.[11]

You are being led into high and lofty places.

You can't be intimidated by others who talk a big talk or do big things. Truly, that's a message I constantly have to preach to myself. You don't have to be intimidated by this journey. More than being equipped, you've been given the peace of Elohim which passes all understanding.[12] His shalom wraps its arms as a big hug around your shoulders, and gives you the peaceful courage to take that first step. You have completion—not competition—in Yeshua, brought to your fullest potential in His power and authority.[13]

So go on, girl- take that first step. You're equipped for it!

11.   Colossians 1:11-12
12.   Philippians 4:7
13.   Colossians 2:10

1. Look up each verse footnoted in this chapter. Write the ones that spoke to your heart below.

2. In the chapter "You Are Gifted," you already wrote down the talents you have. Look back at that list, pray over it, and pick out 1-3 of those talents which truly make you feel alive in your soul and that you know you do well. Do any of these talents have a common golden thread that weaves all the way back to your childhood? List those 1-3 giftings here:

3. Pray over the talent(s) you listed above, and ask Adonai to give you ideas and vision for how He wants you to pursue the use of them. Write down your brainstormed ideas and big-dream visions here:

4. In what ways does the enemy tell you half-truths-full-lies, intimidating you to not even begin pursuing these avenues?

5. With a black pen, draw a line through all the half-truths-full-lies you listed above. Now, write the other half of the truth below, defeating the enemy's schemes. (i.e. ~~"I don't have the money"~~ "Elohim will provide all my needs"). Taking a red pen or highlighter, circle these complete truths.

6. What are some of your fears about your current season of life? How could pursing the talents with which Adonai has equipped you give you renewed purpose and confidence right where you are?

7. Its easy to be distracted by so many things—other people, thoughts, the internet. Think about all the "wasted" moments of your daily life—browsing Pinterest, scrolling Instagram, focusing on what others are doing instead of what *you* should be doing. Identify some time-wasters below, along with more productive substitutes.

8. Write out five goals you need to achieve in order to reach that big brainstorm idea to which you feel Adonai is calling you. Circle the first goal you need to meet. Then, write down one daily task that will help you take steps towards completing that goal.

9. How does knowing you are an ambassador of Yeshua change your life or how you present yourself?

10. In what ways could your pursuit deviate from praising Adonai to glorifying yourself? How can you guard against going down this wrong road?

11. Sometimes we all need to be reminded, "You can do this!" Look back through this chapter to find words that really jumped out in affirmation to you (*Here are a few to get you started: I am... Equipped. Strengthened. Empowered. Complete. Purposeful. Submitted.*) Circle, underline, or highlight these words each place they appear in the chapter. Then, copy these words below in your own handwriting with bold print and multiple colors, a statement to your soul.

CHAPTER SEVEN

You Are An Overcomer

Dear Overcoming You,

You can do this.

The chains may seem too heavy, the struggle may seem too strong, the battle may seem like it could never be won, but the truth is, there is a warrior within.

The same power that raised Yeshua from the grave lives in you.[1]

You are an overcomer, you are more than a conqueror through Adonai's love.[2] This mountain that you face is moved by faith, with doubt drowned to the bottom of the sea. I know it sometimes feels like it will never move, that things will never change—that you can't do this on your own.

And you're right. You can't do this on your own.

Yeshua came to break chains and set prisoners free,[3] and He's standing there holding the keys. He won't force Himself upon you, or take away your free choice.

---

1. Romans 8:11
2. Romans 8:37
3. Luke 4:16-20

But He's standing there, waiting for you to ask.

I don't know what jail cell you've been staying in, whether its Guilt or Fear or Self, but the key that He holds opens them all. He's there to lead you out in triumphal procession in order to reveal to you who you are in Him, spreading the fragrance of His knowledge wherever you go.[4]

He's walking you out of the dominion of darkness and into the Kingdom of light.[5]

I think each of us has a vivid picture of this truth in our lives, but someone who comes to the forefront of my mind is my beautiful friend Gavriella. You name it, Gavi has been through it, and she testifies that a transformation from darkness to light isn't ever a quick relocation. We still have a sin nature that wars with our spirit, a constant battle between right and wrong. It's definitely not easy, and if you ask Gavi, she hesitates to call herself an overcomer because she still deals with the temptations and struggles and the pulls of pressure. Yet, this is what makes her an overcomer. Even though she may stumble, she still chooses to get back up and try again.

Temptation tries to keep her down, but by the power of Yeshua in her, it can't.

She knows that greater is Yeshua living in her than all the adversaries that prowl the world.[6] She recognizes those areas that need extra guarding in her life, and she attacks them with a true warrior spirit. She chooses not to dwell on all the horrible hardships she has endured and painful parts of her story she wishes she didn't have. She knows that she overcomes by the

---

4.   2 Corinthians 2:14
5.   Colossians 1:13
6.   1 John 4:4

blood of the Lamb and the testimony that she has been given.[7] The enemy tries to wave failure in her face, but she knows Who she belongs to. She knows who she is.

Gavi knows she is not common, and neither are you.

We are not common people. We are children of the King of Heaven, the Lover of our Souls. We were not created to succumb to temptation. We were not made to be chained by shame. Gavi knows that she can't guard her heart on her own. She has to allow Adonai to stand in that place while she rests at Yeshua's feet, learning to just be still with Him. She's constantly learning and growing, refusing to settle into a stagnant self. She knows that relapses aren't defeats, they're opportunities to become more confident, more bold, more strong in being an overcomer.

An overcomer presses through failure, no matter how sloppy it may look to outsiders.

I may not have a story quite as dramatic as Gavi, but that's the beauty of each of our unique chapters. We all have tasted similar lessons, while maybe not going through similar circumstances. My overcoming story comes branded in my name—which means "victory"—yet for years it felt like a slap in the face. The enemy used it in his favor to taunt me every time I fell short of the goal. It became a constant reminder of not being good enough, of not being powerful enough to conquer all.

The only victorious conqueror is the one who is submitted to Yeshua...and who lets Him fight the battles.

For years I allowed my name to be my greatest weakness rather than my greatest strength. My middle name—Marie—means "bitterness", and I chose instead to dwell there rather

---

7.   Revelation 12:11

than in bold victory. It wasn't until I was writing my own identity statement when I was twenty-one that I realized I am a victorious overcomer of disappointment and hardship. I didn't have to have bitterness be the victor in my life. I was created to be victorious over bitterness.

I don't have to dwell in the bitter places, because the brand on my soul is that Yeshua's victory triumphs over all.

It's not just my name, it's true of yours, too. Names are so beautifully important, which is why you see Adonai change names all throughout Scripture. Abram's name is changed to Abraham, Sarai's to Sarah, Jacob's to Israel. Regardless of your name and it's meaning, it's being used in your life.

How are you viewing it?

This summer, I was sharing with my friend Jennifer about this book and all that Adonai was teaching me. We were talking about names, and she admitted she didn't like hers at all because of what it meant—"white wave", or basically, a raging wild storm. For Jennifer, it's what her life felt like, and she didn't want to feel tossed around anymore, flailing in the water. However, when I see Jennifer, I see something else.

I see a strong, brave woman, walking on the waves with Yeshua in the midst of every storm that rages in her life.

In Yeshua, Jennifer's "white waves" didn't signal a woman drowning in all the torrents that come her way. It revealed a heart like Peter, stepping out to walk on the waves in faith, knowing that Yeshua is right there if only she keeps her eyes on Him.[8] It's hard to focus on Him when the roar of the waves deafens your hearing and the winds of chaos whip around you. It takes a choice—a choice to not think out of fear and flesh,

---

8.   Matthew 14:22-33

but to believe that we have been given the mind of Messiah.[9]
We are able to ponder the spiritual rather than the physical in
situations like these.

*How does your thinking need to shift in order to view the
Savior instead of focusing on the storm?*

Maybe you feel like your name has always had a negative
meaning, something that keeps you chained down. But I hope
and pray that you're able to see past whatever it may be in
order to take your every thought (and every aspect of your life
and name) captive to the power of Yeshua.[10] Maybe you've felt
like I have, like the meaning of your name was never something
you could achieve and it only brings you lower. Maybe you've
felt like Jennifer, like your name had so much heavy baggage
that you could only sink rather than swim.

*But I'm here to tell you that you are an overcomer, and
you can walk on the water, too.*

Don't carry around a spirit of fear—fear of the future, fear
of failure, fear of the giants armed for war. We have been
equipped with a spirit of power, of love, and of self-discipline.[11]
We are fully capable to quench all the fiery darts of the wicked
one with our shield of faith.[12]

*We ought not to give the enemy more awe and fear than
we do our Creator.*

Many Believers tiptoe around the adversary with such a
trembling in their souls that it's almost superstitious. They

9.   1 Corinthians 2:16
10.   2 Corinthians 10:5
11.   2 Timothy 1:7
12.   Ephesians 6:16

illuminate the enemy's power to kill, steal, and destroy,[13] and underestimate Yeshua's all-conquering power that overcomes all that this world holds.[14]

Do not be overcome by evil, but rather, overcome evil with good.[15]

No darkness can snuff out Yeshua's light,[16] so we are slaves to sin no longer.[17] The old you was chained to a thread of SELF- whether self-harm, self-destruction, self-inflicted eating disorders, or selfish depression over a world that doesn't treat you the way you want. Self has been crucified with Yeshua, so don't spend time trying to resurrect it from the ashes. We are no longer slaves to the flesh, and we have one solution, one victory over it all.

Yeshua.

When you know who you are in Him, your spiritual adrenaline is supercharged to battle for a winning victory with Yeshua at the helm. You take your stand on Adonai's words, claiming His promises that you are far from oppression, and that fear does not come near you.[18]

Claim it because you know it to be true in the depths of your soul.

It's not just nice sounding words, it's your life.[19] Walk in bold confidence that you don't have to succumb to temptations and pulls and lusts any longer. Rise above, empowered by the Holy

---

13.   John 10:10
14.   John 16:33
15.   Romans 12:21
16.   John 1:5
17.   Romans 6:6
18.   Isaiah 54:14
19.   Deuteronomy 32:47

Spirit. Know that through Yeshua you have victory over all the power of the enemy, and nothing shall harm you. You are a Kingdom weapon, wielded in the hands of Adonai to heal the sick and cast out demons and to speak in tongues.[20]

Who wants to stay swaddled in sin when you could be living in powerful, Kingdom-shaping victory?

Everything in life is a choice, and I think you already know what to choose. I don't know what temptations are tearing at your soul. I don't know what hard situations you're going through, the ones that make you feel like you'll never come out from the valley. I don't know if your current battlefield is in your mind or your heart or your physical life. But please, don't wait. Don't put it off for another day, don't you dare say you're not able to conquer this.[21] Start tackling those temptations and shedding the "self."

The power of Yeshua in you can defeat all the giants if you'll choose to work with Him to do so.

20.   Mark 16:17-18
21.   Philippians 4:13

1. Look up each verse footnoted in this chapter. Write the ones that spoke to your heart below.

2. What mountain (whether physical, spiritual, a circumstance or temptation) are you facing in your life? In what ways have you allowed it to rule over you, instead of allowing Yeshua to rule over all that you are?

3. There once was a man who lived in a village surrounded by treacherous cliffs and unscalable mountain walls. In order to reach his village, you had to take a thirty-two mile walk around the mountain's spine, which meant medical help and supplies were very limited. One day, this man's wife stumbled on the sharp path and as a result of no available medical attention she died. Yet this man didn't allow the mountain to defeat him. Every morning, he arose early in the morning with his chisel in hand, and attacked the side of the mountain fervently until he would have to leave for work. His fellow villagers thought he was crazy— no one could possibly move a mountain! Yet, he persisted, every day, year after year. Twenty-two years later Dashrath Manjhi successfully chiseled out a safe and smooth pathway through the Gehlaur hills. His daily persistence, his refusal to be defeated by discouragement, and his commitment to hard work paid off, both for his village and for future travelers. What is one daily task YOU need to do in order to move the mountain that's in your way?

4. What would your life look like and how would you feel
    with this mountain removed? Expound your feelings of
    hope below. Keep these thoughts at the forefront of your
    mind as a motivation to keep chiseling away!

5. On a sticky note, write "I am not common". Stick it in a
    place that will remind you whenever you are faced with
    temptation (the fridge, your computer, the bathroom,
    your journal) that you can rise above. You are not
    common like everyone else who allows themselves to
    succumb to defeat. You belong to Adonai, and there is
    nothing common about that!

6. Look up the meanings of your first, middle, and (if
    possible) last name. Write the meanings below.

7. Pray over your names' meanings, and see how they can be arranged to declare a deeper meaning and a story of Elohim's sovereignty, plan, and purpose for your life. Take my name as an example: "I am a victorious overcomer (Victoria) of bitterness (Marie) as a warrior who pursues peace (Humphrey)." Write yours below.

8. Does your name have a negative connotation to it? If so, how have you been living in this negativity rather than allowing Yeshua to redeem your name?

9. Share a situation where you gave the enemy greater fear and respect than you gave Yeshua. Now, knowing of and believing in Yeshua's power over all darkness and evil, how would you have responded differently?

10. Re-read Mark 16:17-18. In what ways does this change your view of being a disciple of Yeshua? How does it change your life?

11. In what ways have you allowed your sinful nature to rule over you? List them below, then share these with a Godly person (perhaps one of the ones you approached in the chapter "You Are Gifted") and ask to be held accountable in these areas.

12. List the choices you need to make in order to conquer the temptations that desire your soul.

CHAPTER EIGHT

You Are Royalty

Dear Royal You,

Playing princess wasn't just for your carefree childhood.

Somehow along the way, life hits you hard in the face and tries to steal all the innocence you've ever possessed. It's out to steal your joy and leave you feeling worthless. It leaves you the last person picked for a sports team, it leaves you sitting alone while the rest of the party mingles, it leaves you awkwardly left out of inside jokes.

It leaves you shaken of any confidence you once had and kicks you to the curb of insecurity.

For most of my life, I was an extremely insecure person. Always feeling overshadowed by someone else's fame, feeling like I could never cast a light bright enough to steal the show. I remember hearing stories being shared of cousins and siblings, nieces and nephews, distant relatives and close friends who were making it big and were worthy of excited conversation by grandparents, parents, aunts and uncles. But me? The conversation on that topic seemed so quick and insignificant compared to everyone else's accomplishments.

*It scarred me so deeply that I couldn't ever confidently
share anything about myself the rest of my youth.*

A couple years ago, I was standing in the kitchen with a new
friend who asked what I did with my time. I hesitated, fumbled
with some silverware on the counter and randomly opened
cabinets while I mumbled a quick and rather weak summary.
I shrugged my shoulders as I finished, a kind of retreat away
from any comments that might come forth. What happened
next I never expected.

Mama Bear was in the kitchen too.

My mom set the record straight, not just for my friend,
but for myself. Listening to her list all the things I actually do
in a day, all the projects in which I'm involved, all the people
to whom I reach out, left me speechless. Did I really do all
that? The way she talked made me sound so important that I
wondered how I could have ever doubted my worth before.

*But without Yeshua as your designated Definer, the world
easily defines you.*

The world will tell you that you need a college education,
that you need to get a job, that you really should move out and
start dating just to have experience. It tells you that a mother
should effortlessly manage a full-time job, Pinterest-perfect
house, and raise model children. It tells you being a princess
isn't enough, that you've got to leave the castle to show it all
and be appreciated by everyone else. When you don't measure
up to their checklists, it can be hard to justify your priorities or
substitute a worthy enough price tag.

*Unless you are rooted in Yeshua, His priorities for your
life will never seem enough compared to what the world
wants you to do.*

When I was twenty-one, I did something completely bold and brave and out of my comfort zone. I stepped alone onto a plane bound for Israel, totally terrified of what I was doing and honestly, with no confidence in who I truly was. I was leaving behind the people I leaned on—my parents and a few close friends—whose words of worth and encouragement had become my crutches to move me forward in any given direction.

Talk about going cold turkey.

There I was, on the other side of the world, coming face to face with all my insecurities. It wasn't just the spiritual and emotional aspect, it was physically, too. I was pushed around on the Temple Mount, sick every week, nearly blown off the mountain during a horrible wind storm that swung the walls of the building out so that I saw the sunlight crack through along the floor. I was living amongst two hundred other people in close quarters, and those weak walls definitely had ears, so I wasn't about to indulge in any heart-to-hearts via FaceTime with my mother. I missed my flight home due to the worst stomach bug I'd ever had in my life, and caught another international flight by myself less than twenty-four hours after—being honest here—what felt like puking my guts up.

So much for all the warm motivational speeches I was used to. It was just me and Adonai, staring at my suitcase of insecurities, labels, and all the politically correct (and incorrect) things I felt I needed to measure up to.

Perhaps you've experienced something similar, something where you felt like you were being stretched beyond your capacity to withstand, and you were face-to-face with the Creator of your soul over all the baggage weighing you down. Once content to be the princess of the castle, you have listened as many other voices have called you out and told you what you should do in order to be productive and purposeful. You left your princess crown to journey for identity and worth, and you've gathered up so many heavy trinkets along the way. Looking into your overflowing bag, you wonder, "Does the beauty of these things define me? Or are all these cheap tchotchkes reflecting my worth to the world—broken, plastic, and without value?"

This is a serious identity crisis at the crossroads of the world and His Word.

The world says one thing, Yeshua declares another. In all the noisy chaos, He asks you to calm your soul and just listen for His still, small voice to lead you home.[1] He knows it's a lot to process and absorb, this acceptance of all the beauty He's created in your soul. I don't know about your crisis, but it's taken me (literally) years to process that Israel trip where Adonai stripped me of all the labels I had allowed others to stick on me. He showed up in such powerful ways, in such deep layers that I couldn't comprehend right then, but looking back now, I do.

At the crux of it all, my suitcase was heavy, and Yeshua wanted me to let go of the handles, and instead, hold onto His truth, and to trade it back for a crown.[2]

In search for what the world tells us is a greater scheme, we forget that we are no longer slaves. We are children of Elohim, and not only that, but we are heirs of the Kingdom.[3] There is no other place where we so securely belong. While the world challenges us to make our voices heard and to set up monuments of our accomplishments, we must hold tightly to our passports which say our citizenship is in Heaven.[4]

1.   1 Kings 19:11-12
2.   Revelation 3:11
3.   Galatians 4:7
4.   Philippians 3:20

When you realize that, it's not necessary to travel the world to find your roots.

It's a mystery the way Adonai works, each of our journeys shrouded in misty unknown. It's a mystery that through the Gospel, we are heirs together with Israel, members together of one body, sharers together in Yeshua's promises.[5] I don't claim to know how it all works, how we all have Abraham as our forefather and are heirs with him to the promises.[6]

But one thing I know—that's a genealogy I'm holding onto.

My identity isn't something that is up for debate. It's not something that friends or strangers or family members can take away. You and I, we are a part of a chosen generation, royal and holy and purchased, and nonreturnable.[7] We are Elohim's children, born again of the incorruptible seed of the Word of God which lives and abides forever and isn't going to expire.[8] We receive, we believe, we have this right and it's something you can bank on. [9]

Adonai has defined us as His, and nothing can reverse His declaration that we are heirs with Messiah.[10]

Just as Yeshua's title of Messiahship isn't going away anytime soon, neither is ours. We are called to be saints, belonging to the congregation of Elohim, sanctified in Yeshua, united with all those who call out to Him.[11] It's a royal court, surrounded by many mighty ones in faith. We belong here in

5.   Ephesians 3:6
6.   Galatians 3:29
7.   1 Peter 2:9
8.   1 Peter 1:23
9.   John 1:12
10. Romans 8:17
11. 1 Corinthians 1:2

the midst of them, not as a servant, or someone low down on the ladder. No, Yeshua calls us friends, and reveals the King's heart to us in a beautifully intimate way.[12]

Why would we ever want to belong to anything or anyone else, when the Maker of the galaxies claims us as His own, and invites us to partake in His divine nature?[13] Why would we seek any other way of escaping the corruption and confusion the world wants to shove down our throats?

Through Yeshua, we reign in life through Elohim's abundant provision of grace and righteousness,[14] which are His overflowing treasures saved for us. The world may want to throw us to the ground, yet we are raised with Yeshua and made to sit in heavenly places with Him.[15]

We are born of Elohim. We are royalty. The enemy can't touch us.[16]

There is so much freedom and empowerment in that thought. If you and I are defined by Adonai, if we take up our position in His royal court with gladness, if we are confident in the crown we wear, then we are unstoppable. No pull or pressure from the world can shake us down. No insecurity or lie or deception in our minds are allowed to take root, because we stand firmly upon these promises. We don't need the affirmation or approval or dictation from any other, because we have but one King who rules our hearts, one King we answer to, only one King Whose approval we seek.

---

12.   John 15:15
13.   2 Peter 1:3-4
14.   Romans 5:17
15.   Ephesians 2:6
16.   1 John 5:18

We are free to dance for the audience of One.

So keep your chin up and your crown on, Princess. You belong to El Shaddai. There is no question and no uncertainty as to Whom you belong.

Your royal worth is far above rubies.[17]

---

17. Proverbs 31:10

1.   Look up each verse footnoted in this chapter. Write the
       ones that spoke to your heart below.

2.   Before you even start into the rest of the questions, do
       yourself a little favor. Make yourself a cup of tea (what's
       more royal than that?!) and put on a piece of jewelry. Take
       a little time to fix your hair in a stylish way. Sometimes
       it's hard to remember you're royalty when you've spent
       the week living in pajamas or a grungy jean skirt, so give
       yourself a physical reminder by taking a few moments to
       put yourself together. You are royalty, you are an heir of
       the Kingdom, so it is perfectly acceptable to dress like it!

3.   How has insecurity held you back from pursuing the
       dreams Elohim has placed in your heart?

4. In the past, who have you allowed to define you? How did it make you feel, and how did it work out?

5. How does Yeshua define you, and how can you live confidently in that freedom?

6. List all the labels you've allowed others to stick on your soul. Next to these harmful labels, list all the labels that Yeshua writes on your soul instead (preferably opposite of the harmful label, i.e. "Unworthy" and "Worthy"). Spend some time praying for deliverance and cleansing from these harmful labels you've been carrying, and then blot each harmful one out with a black marker. Next, circle each of Yeshua's labels He speaks to your soul with a red pen, symbolizing His blood that bought you and has a right to define you. This is your new royal definition!

7. Purchase (or make!) a tiara/crown. Whenever you start to feel like the enemy's labels are sticking in your mind again, stand in front of the mirror with your tiara on and read out loud Yeshua's labels that you wrote above.

8. What have you allowed to become a "crutch" you use to get through life? What are some clear steps you are going to take to walk on your own, confident as a princess of Adonai?

9. In this chapter, I shared how I went to Israel and came face to face with all my insecurities in the midst of hardships. Have you ever had a similar experience where it was just you, Adonai, and the baggage you were carrying (even figuratively)? Share the experience below, as well as the lesson you learned from it.

10. How does it change the way you live, speak, and the choices you make, to know that your citizenship is not of this world, but is in Heaven?

11. In John 15:15, we read that Yeshua desires to share with us the things Elohim has revealed to Him. What are some things that you want to be revealed to you? List them below, then spend time praying that He would open your eyes to behold the truths you seek.

12. 1 John 5:18 says that the enemy cannot touch us. Draw a box around those words in your Bible, a reminder that when we walk in holiness, we have nothing to fear!

CHAPTER NINE

You Are Healed

Dear Healed You,

Stop picking your scabs open.

I know, I sound like your mother. As a child, that was a phrase I heard often. I was a notorious scab-picker, scraping and irritating my healing skin until oftentimes it would bleed over and over again. I'd peel and pick and pull, as if each scab was an invitation for more destruction rather than restoration. Because the itch of the healing scab seemed like too much to ignore, my attempts to remedy the feeling only left my skin more raw and tender than before.

If I had trusted the healing process, I wouldn't have needed the countless extra bandaids, tubes of antibacterial cream, and I wouldn't carry dozens of scars.

When we don't like the healing process, our attempts to speed the process often only set back our progress. In our impatience, we don't want to endure the momentary unpleasantness, so in exchange for a thorough healing we expose our wounds again and again with our own two hands.

A wound can't heal when it's constantly irritated.

I don't know how you've been hurt. Maybe emotionally, maybe spiritually, maybe physically. My heart hurts right along with you, because you've walked through some hard things. Whether you have scabs and callouses over your heart or your eyes because of it, I'm praying that this chapter ministers to your soul.

You are healed in Yeshua.

I don't know what hard thing you're going through now, but for me as I write this, mine is finding out my brother is experiencing end of life symptoms as cancer entwines within his body. You and I may be going through totally different experiences, but one thing remains: Our situations call for so much prayer, and sometimes we feel ill-equipped to do it.

But we already know that we are equipped in Yeshua. Our weakness is an opportunity for His strength.

We must never forget that even in the hard things, God has GOOD things in store for us. Every piece of this complicated, chaotic puzzle is shaped specifically to fit with the next. You can trust that any circumstance you're walking through where you feel it's just too far gone to be brought back to beauty will fit perfectly into His masterpiece. It seems so distant right now, so far off, but you can trust His love. You can trust His heart. You can trust His hand.

If we're not trusting, then what a lousy attitude we have regarding Elohim's love. It's shortsighted to only think the bad things in life come from Him.

If we observe others around us—even those who aren't believers—moving through different situations, you'll notice a pattern and theme around their responses. When things go well, people will attribute it to "happy coincidence," but when things go badly, such as death or loss or sickness, people ask, "Why did Elohim allow this?"

Is this our response to pain?

The truth is, we serve a good, good Father who loves to give good gifts to His children! We say life isn't a bed of roses, but I think it is. There is beauty, but there are thorns, too. The hard times that Adonai does allow, He only allows for our ultimate good: to draw us deeper into His heart and to be purified.

He wants a pure bride, but He also has a soft spot for a good love story.

I think part of the reason we go through trials and pain is because of the story we will have at the end. Adonai loves stories—that's why we're commanded to tell our children and grandchildren of what happened to our forefathers in the wilderness, the entire story of the exodus from Egypt.[1]

There is power in our stories—in your story—for the glory of His great name.

If we think about it, isn't that what Scripture is? An entire book filled with stories and love. His love letter to us, our love back to Him. Our pain and sickness, Yeshua's power to bind up every wound.

Yeshua, wounded, bruised, and chastised for us, and by His stripes we are healed.[2]

Maybe your physical healing doesn't come. For my brother, it's been seven years of aggressive cancer and over eighty rounds of chemo, the loss of a lung and multiple surgeries on his brain, and the healing still hasn't come. For me, it's been a lifelong struggle with a weakened immune system due to being born with e-coli. For my friend Sierra (remember her from chapter "Dear Beautiful You"?), it is blindness.

1.   Exodus 12:26-27
2.   Isaiah 53:5

*But we don't focus on the injustice, because this world is
not our home.*

We can be healed in our body but live with souls crippled
by bitterness and smeared with ugly anger. Regardless of our
physical circumstances, what will we choose–to allow Elohim
to be the ultimate Healer or to continue to pick our scabs open
until our hearts are calloused and deformed?

*We have died to sin and live in righteousness, healed by
a Messiah whose body bore the marks so that our hearts
wouldn't have to.*[3]

When I think of healing, my joyful friend Naomi comes to
mind. She bubbles laughter and joy into every conversation,
she jumps in to help out with any project, and is one of the most
gifted Hebrew teachers I know of. I had known Naomi for years,
but never knew her story until I was in the midst of a Hebrew
lesson she was teaching. While the class was overwhelmed
and despairing at our lack of progress from our very beginner
perspective, Naomi pulled from the story Adonai had given
her, and related it to us.

Naomi knew her story—her pain—wasn't without purpose.

You see, before knowing Hebrew, Naomi became sick
and was completely paralyzed for two years. She couldn't do
anything for herself. She depended on others to feed her, brush
her hair, take care of her. Through her bedridden season, she
applied herself to learning Hebrew in whatever ways she could.
She couldn't write it, she couldn't flip a page, but she could
listen. Her paralysis wasn't an obstacle to her hearing, so she
spent hours listening to Hebrew. She didn't let her sickness
stop her from living life with purpose.

---

3.   1 Peter 2:24

*She took the hard story Elohim had given her and chose
to be as intentional as she could to see the good.*

Naomi's story of learning—and eventual healing—is so
powerful to my heart. I've been a "quitter" for too long. When
things get tough, my first inclination is to succumb to defeat.
My first response isn't to trust the healing process or to redeem
the time; instead, I balk and hide and run away from the pain
instead of embracing the healing that will come through it.
Naomi's testimony challenges me to push on through the
pain, to see purpose in it, to press in to Adonai's heart and
press on to pursue victory.

*Our greatest victories can emerge from paths of pain, and
our deepest joys are forged in the fire of trial.*

When I think of the happiest people I know of, all of them
have walked through tough things. Abuse, poverty, death,
homelessness, physical infirmities, chronic illness. Their joy
isn't dependent on physical things anymore, because they
know from experience how quickly circumstances can change.

They bank their joy on Yeshua, because He alone is constant.

Yeshua shows up in the middle of the pain, in the middle
of the chaos. He extends His Own wounded hands to close
and heal the wounds of your heart. He takes His scalpel all in
love and scrapes away all the infection of pride and festering of
anger. He removes the hard tumors of bitterness and doesn't
stop the surgery until He is confident of success.

Yeshua isn't a quitter. He finishes the story that He writes.[4]

And when the surgery is complete, you begin to see how
a once hard, even bitter experience has been transformed into
one of light and hope. Looking back over the story of your life,
you no longer see the pain, but the purpose.

---

4.   Hebrews 12:2

Instead of resisting, trust the healing.

In my own life, it's the deepest hurts and the hardest experiences that have drawn me close to the heart of Elohim. Our bodies carry physical scars, but I know our souls carry spiritual scars, too. There is healing in the name of Yeshua, but not all is erased. Scars remain, but you see those differently now, too. Just like stretch marks on a new mother, they reveal growth and beauty and life anew.

He leaves the scars in order for you to remember His stories.

1. Look up each verse footnoted in this chapter. Write the ones that spoke to your heart below.

2. What situations in your life are you constantly irritating by trying to fix them your way, instead of letting Adonai do the healing?

3. What would these situations look like if you trusted Adonai and His ways of healing?

4. In the middle of such difficult situations, it's hard to remember that Adonai only does things for our ultimate good (Romans 8:28). In the situations you mentioned above, what could be some good things Adonai brings forth in your life through experiencing these hard situations? What character traits is He growing in your life through these things?

5. What kind of attitude toward Adonai's love do you have? How has that perspective shifted after reading this chapter?

6. Think over your life and the people you've met. Has there been a person whose story really impacted you? Share their story below, and why it impacted your heart.

7. Think over your own life story. What might the highlights
    be, as well as the lowlights? At the end of your days, what
    do you hope your story and legacy will say?

8. If you don't already, consider keeping a journal to record
    the ways Adonai is working in your life. At the end of each
    day, write the ways He has proven His faithfulness in your
    life. It could be as simple as a convenient parking spot at
    the grocery store, or as big as a breakthrough answer to
    prayer. Collect each and every moment, soaking up the
    radiance of His goodness.

9. In what ways does your soul need healing? How will you
    allow Yeshua to enter into these tender places to do His
    work? Write out a prayer below, inviting Him to begin the
    process and stating what your hopes are for healing.

10. Answer honestly: Are you most often a quitter or a victor? Knowing that Yeshua finishes the things He starts, how does it motivate you?

11. What scars do you carry that testify to Elohim's redeeming power? What stories of His faithfulness do they tell? How can you choose to focus on the stories of these scars rather than on the pain of them?

12. What are some of your greatest victories that were forged in the paths of pain?

CHAPTER TEN

You Are Beloved

Dear Beloved You,

No love could satisfy as deeply as the love of Elohim.

The One who created your beating heart, Who knows every rhythmic pattern it produces and every longing that emerges, is the One Who sustains you in order to love you more deeply and fully.

A man may try to understand your heart's workings, but no one can know it so completely as Adonai.

Many girls look longingly for that mysterious age—whether sixteen or eighteen or twenty-one—that they feel holds the gateway to romance. It's a season that eludes and nearly always disappoints, a season filled with confusion and dashed expectations.

Instead of living as accepted and loved today,[1] we imagine it only comes in the future.

I understand the struggle, the desire for a lover and a home of your own. It's a holy desire, woven within our frame, a righteous calling on our lives. It's what we were created for, to be a helper, the very thing that is the cause of womankind's existence.[2]

1. Ephesians 1:6
2. Genesis 2:18

Something so deeply intimate and personal, we imagine life would be perfection once we reach that season. That this call is the sole purpose of why we're here on planet earth.

The truth is, Yeshua, not marriage, is our life, and we will be revealed with Him in glory.[3]

Adonai is such a generous Elohim that He did not create our lives for the mundane. He created us with purpose and passion and pursuits, He created us with distinct identity and unique values. He gives us hopeful vision and a beautiful future.[4]

That's not all. He gives us a meaningful and impactful today, too.

Adonai is not out to love you for who you will be, but for who you are now.[5] So lavish is His love over you, that He removes every obstacle and label and barrier that separates you from being together with Yeshua.[6] Oh yes, the future is bright and glorious, and perhaps it holds an earthly love story all its own, but that glow of hope can't quench the epic romance He's wooing your heart with today.

What if you lived this reality of being lavishly loved now, rather than waiting for the future?

How would life look if you lived as one who truly belongs to Yeshua, knowing that every moment of your day He desires your heart?[7] What is your response to an Elohim who is rich in mercy and who is compelled by His great immeasurable love for you?[8]

---

3.   Colossians 3:4
4.   Jeremiah 29:11
5.   Romans 5:8
6.   Galatians 3:28-29
7.   Song of Songs 7:10
8.   Ephesians 2:4-5

I don't know about you, but I'd live in celebration if I truly understood this.

I'd attend everyone else's wedding with wild excitement, dancing with Yeshua and dressed in my very best, instead of sadness that it's not my "special day." I'd grab a latte and go for a walk with Adonai downtown, talking about what's going on in my life and not minding that there's no earthly beau walking next to me. I'd wake up excited every day in anticipation of how He will reveal more of His love to me. I'd live without fear of the future or fear of singlehood because I no longer live life chained by it. Rather, I'm hidden, safe, and protected, with Yeshua.[9]

I'd live knowing I am perfectly loved by Him instead of waiting to be loved by Mr. Right.

I love what my friend Hannah does. She is single, but she lives life celebrating all the little things that come into her day. It doesn't take much for her heart to explode in praise, and I truly think its because she focuses on living a great life, right here, right now.

Living loved. Being beloved.

One thing that Hannah did stood out to me in a big way. One evening, she decided to go to a sit-down restaurant while she was running errands in town. She walked in, asked for a table for one, and held her chin up while the hostess gave her a look of pity. While other couples noticed her walking alone into the room, she determined she wouldn't allow wishful thinking to ruin her evening. Don't misunderstand. She longs to be married. Of course, deep down or in the way back corners of her mind, she wants a table for two instead of for one.

---

9.   Colossians 3:3

But she choses to live loved and invites her Beloved to join her.

I haven't gone to a restaurant by myself yet, but after hearing Hannah's story, it's on my list. Hannah made a statement to herself and to the world that evening: she wasn't going to wait in sadness while she could live with joy—a message that can be applied to everyone, no matter what season you're in. She had a beautiful evening, relaxing and enjoying the solitude to reevaluate things that were going on in her life. She lives the life Adonai has given her with joy, even if it doesn't look the way she always dreamed it would.

She knows that she is united with Yeshua, one in Spirit, together in love.[10]

Perhaps its because I've fallen head over heels in love with the vineyards of Israel, but Yeshua's fruit and vine metaphor in John 15 woos my heart every time. The concept of being rooted in the place Adonai has you, to drink deeply of the Holy Spirit, to abide with Yeshua on the vine, it's all such a beautiful word picture of how to grow fruitful and rapidly in love with Him.

Love is hard—beautifully hard—in every way. It's a dance of giving and receiving, a life lived open and vulnerable.

Being beloved doesn't mean that things will be easy, but it does mean that there is an anchor in life's storms.[11] For singles, we may only picture the happiness that marriage brings, but the reality of marriage is life continues to have challenging chapters (and all the married women say, "Amen!"). There's losing jobs and babies born, there's moving to another state, there's sicknesses and hard days, there's deaths of loved ones and new seasons of growth. Yet, we don't focus on the changes or the hard things up ahead.

10.   1 Corinthians 6:17
11.   Hebrews 6:19

We'd go anywhere and do anything for the man we love.

Even in all the chaos, there's a safe feeling in love. Even in the sacrificing and hard days, there's a sure foundation underneath our feet—a covenant in place, a *ketubah*[12] signed. A declaration of "I'm with you, no matter what comes our way."

Yeshua commits the same to us. He paid the bride price on the cross.

Neither death nor life cannot separate us. No powers or principalities, nothing today and nothing tomorrow. No matter the height or depth of the situation, nothing—yes, nothing— can separate us from the love of Adonai expressed through Yeshua.[13] As for us, love means staying on the vine, abiding in His love, no matter what the weather conditions are or what plague comes our way.[14]

It's taking in the Spirit and giving back our lives to the One Who gave us all.

I hope that by now, reading this far into this book, you've come face to face with all the promises made toward you in Scripture and see the love and delight that Adonai seeks to lavish on you. I hope you recognize that every proclamation and word of life He speaks over you comes straight from His heart to yours.

Everything is motivated out of love.

That's what my friend Marili likes to say, and when she does it causes me to stop and think hard about what my motives are in every situation. If it was love that motivated Yeshua to die

---

12. Jewish marriage contract, outlining the covenant and commitment of
      the bride and groom.
13. Romans 8:38-39
14. John 15:9

for me, if it was love that motivated Him to redeem me and set me free...shouldn't I reciprocate that love with every breath I breathe?

No matter the situation, the people, the confrontation, shouldn't love be seen in me?

It's an easy concept when life is peachy keen and the world is cheery. It's an entirely different matter when friends betray you, when your heart is taken advantage of, when you're picked last for the play, or when you don't make the team.

What will your next step—your response—in these circumstances be? Will it be motivated by love?

I had that challenge recently. Several friends of mine were chosen for a really awesome job in an organization I dearly love. Although I was happy for them, part of me felt a little left out. Left behind. Overlooked. Like no matter how much I give or how much I do, I'm never noticed. Here I am in the corner, while there they are, taking the world by storm.

That's a hard place for a go-getter, big-picture, visionary like me to be.

I'm sure you've been in that place, too. I don't know what you did in your situation, but I knew right then that I needed to be motivated by the love Adonai has lavished on me—not motivated by disappointment. I wrote letters to each of those girls, congratulating them from the sincerity of my heart.

I could rejoice with those who rejoice, because we all are together as one.[15]

---

15.   Romans 12:15

My focus can't be on the giant that wants to drag me into self-defeat, but rather on the Elohim Who conquers all and is in all.[16] The truth is, the place where He has me is GOOD because it's from Him. The place where He has my friends is GOOD because it's from Him.

So let's all sing Kum-Ba-Yah and meet with joy in the middle.

In whatever season you are, I hope you can see that you are so beloved by Elohim, and this strong, passionate, never-ending love is bringing you through it. Even through the disappointment. Through the hurt. Through the gladness and in the sorrow His love is bringing you through. All things work together for our good...because of love.[17]

What will you do to celebrate that beautiful reality today?

16. Ephesians 4:6
17. Romans 8:28

1. Look up each verse footnoted in this chapter. Write the ones that spoke to your heart below.

2. Did you ever have a mental picture of the "ideal gateway" age or season for romance? Describe how you envisioned it to be, and how it has proven to be a letdown.

3. Knowing that Yeshua—not marriage—is the focus of your life, how does that influence your desires and ideals to become a wife and mother? How would this focus impact your husband and children?

4. How is Adonai giving you opportunities and purpose to live an abundant and meaningful life now as a single (or married!) woman? How could these opportunities be a gateway to a hopeful and beautiful future?

5. In this chapter, I shared some ideas of how I would live out being lavishly loved and what my friend Hannah does to remind herself of being beloved. Share below how YOUR life would look if you chose to live lavishly loved and beloved.

6. What are three bold, beautiful things you could do this week to celebrate Yeshua's love over you?

7. Spend some time reading John 15. Journal the words the Holy Spirit impresses on your heart as you meditate on the concept of abiding in Yeshua's love. Underline important verses in your Bible. Circle the words (such as "abide" and "love") that stand out with poignant meaning.

8. How do you rate your ability to abide in Yeshua? What is the fruit in your life that shows you abide in Him? In what ways do you wish to bear more of this fruit in your life, and what needs to change so that you have more uninterrupted time abiding in His presence?

9. Many married couples hang their marriage contract—their ketubah—on their wall as a daily reminder of the foundational trust in their marriage. Sometimes, we also need the physical reminder that Adonai gives us a covenantal love that cannot be shaken. Create a ketubah (look online for ideas!), and write out Romans 8:38-39 on it, as well as any other verses that confirm to your heart the depth of His love over you. Next, write out Ruth 1:16 underneath as a reminder of your commitment to this covenantal love. Sign your name on it, date it, and hang it above your bed. His banner over you is LOVE (Song of Songs 2:4).

10. Write down a hard situation you're in—maybe it's an illness, the betrayal of a friend, a failing grade, or a major disappointment.

11. What is your normal response to this situation? What would your response be if you were motivated by love?

12. Name a current opportunity you have to rejoice with a friend. How will you allow Yeshua's love to overflow through you into this person's life and genuinely celebrate with them?

CHAPTER ELEVEN

You Are Holy

Dear Holy You,

There is glory in His presence.

It's so easy to let shame cloud our view, to allow past mistakes and choices to hold us back from moving forward. The lies of the enemy shout so loud in our ears: *"You're too far gone. There's no hope for you. Holiness is out of reach. There's no redemption here."* We try not to listen, but the words still seep into our consciousness, keeping us living in circles of negativity instead of climbing above such lies.

The lie is that we are too dirty for Adonai to hold.

What a smack in Yeshua's face when we wallow in our sin, and never press forward to claim every promise that His death provided. The enemy wants to hold us back, keep us chained, keep us in the fire but withhold the refining.

I claim this promise to defeat the schemes of the enemy: I am holy and without blame before Adonai in love.[1]

Those aren't my words. They aren't created for a good motivational speech. They're a promise straight from His heart to yours and mine, a concrete concept of our existence.

---

1. Ephesians 1:4

We don't have to live in the pig pits anymore.

If anyone deserved to *not* have a second chance, it would be the prodigal son.[2] He cashes in his tangible inheritance rather than seeking the lessons of his father's legacy. He skips out on responsibility, leaves home and the safety of his orthodox community in order to live wild and free in a pagan nation. No self-control, no more morals, no more restraint, no more need for rules. He spends every last hard-earned coin that his father had saved on a lifestyle that would break his father's heart.

It's ironic that he ends up where he does, considering the extremely un-kosher life he's been living.

Our personal ideals end up manifesting somehow in our lives. The prodigal son's wild and free life lands him living a grotesque life next to the filth of pigs and the reminders of how far he's drifted from religion.

His un-kosher lifestyle manifests in the physical reality of dwelling among un-kosher animals, and it brings the realization that there's not much difference between the two.

You'd think the prodigal son would be classified as too far gone. You'd think he'd bring down his father's head to the grave in sorrow, as a blot on the family name that could never be erased—thanks to the snickering tittle-tattle and disgusted gossip of neighbors and friends. Irredeemable might be the fitting label. Disgrace and shame would be fitting definitions, certainly.

One doesn't expect him to ever recover.

Yet, there in the pig pits, his strong will is broken within him. We don't see the arrogant son, but a humbled son who

---

2.   Luke 15:11-32

can't yet bear to look at his reflection in the mire and face all that he really is. He sees the dishonor, the heavy burden of sin, how unworthy he is of any good thing ever again in his life.

I don't know about you, but I've been there, too.

I've been in that place where I can't forgive myself for the things I've done. I've avoided the mirror, as if a glance would dangerously reveal my marred soul. I'm guessing you've been there, too. You may have felt that you just can't go any lower—since the pig pits are about as low as one could ever go.

Yet, the story concludes with the prodigal son wearing a royal robe, bejeweled and handsome, sitting at the greatest banquet his father has ever thrown.

This son never saw that coming. He certainly didn't see his worth that way. He tried pushing it away, saying again how he wasn't worthy to be counted as a son. He was listening to those inner demons of doubt rather than the words of compassion and love his father was whispering in his ear.

Faced with a choice, he had to let go of the giants of guilt in order to slip his arms into robes of royalty.

He was once in darkness, now living as a child of light.[3] We have a lot in common with the prodigal son, which is why I believe Yeshua made it a point to share this parable. Each one of us, broken in humility, contrite in spirit, have to come face-to-face with the response of overwhelming grace. It is a grace that is intended to shatter every chain of shame and empower us to never live the lifestyle of sin again.[4]

---

3.   Ephesians 5:8
4.   Romans 6:1-2

It is a grace that empowers us to walk in holiness as once broken souls, now beautifully renewed.

It takes a mindset adjustment, a final defeat to the enemy to say he can no longer dictate the rumors whispered to your heart. The truth is, you have been made new in the attitude of your mind. You are a new being, created to be like Elohim in true righteousness and holiness.[5]

We were created for holiness, not shame.

We either walk in the freedom of forgiveness or we don't. We either press on towards the goal and upward call of Elohim in Yeshua,[6] or we stay stagnant.

We either walk out in holiness, or we stay stumbling in the pig pits.

It's a choice of our hearts and minds. We are not chained to the past. We are believers, not doubters, and the light of the Gospel shines in our minds.[7] This holiness, it finds its mark inside and it blazes forward into everything we touch and everyone we meet.

It's a consuming transformation.

By the power that enables Yeshua to bring everything under His control, this same power will transform our lowly bodies so that we will be like His glorious one.[8] Its power is sparking through all aspects of your life and changing you every day to look more like the Son of Elohim.

---

5.   Ephesians 4:23-24
6.   Philippians 3:14
7.   2 Corinthians 4:4
8.   Philippians 3:21

What could be more holy or humbling than that?

Oh, but He's not done. Elohim doesn't stop there, doesn't just transform you from the inside. He states that you are His elect, His chosen, holy and beloved, clothed in tender mercies. He robes you in kindness, humility, meekness, and long-suffering.[9]

Like the prodigal son's father, He decks you out in royal robes, and slides rich rubies of grace upon your fingers.

Even when life hits you hard and you find the mud trailing on your skirt, in every situation ask to be lifted above the mire to be preserved and sanctified for Yeshua.[10] When we view situations as launching pads rather than sinkholes of quicksand, we are driven to achieve more of Him, less of us, and to take that highway of holiness no matter the cost.[11]

We have been given the Holy Spirit, not just as a comforter and a teacher, but literally as a spirit of holiness.[12]

When you feel the conviction of the Holy Spirit, it is the Spirit of Elohim in you recognizing that the situation you are in is a threat to holiness. That feeling when you walk into a place of temptation and you feel the prick in your soul, that innate feeling that this place or these people or that situation is not of Adonai, is a reminder that everywhere you go, He goes too. He cannot stand among the impure.

9.   Colossians 3:12
10. 1 Thessalonians 5:23
11. Isaiah 35:8
12. John 14:26

Holy Spirit conviction reminds you that you are a doer of the Word, and you will be blessed in your actions if you choose to walk in holiness.[13]

It's a reminder that holiness is to be seared in your vision of how you view yourself, how you view the world, and how you view others. My amazing friend Joy once told me an experience she had that will forever be imprinted in my mind as a picture of holiness in everyday life. One day as she was praying outside, wrestling through some tough issues going on in her life, she heard Yeshua speaking to her, saying, *"Look at the sun."* Doubtful she heard right, she began to reason a way around it, but she only heard the command repeated again. So there an obedient Joy stood, staring at the sun with eyes burning from its intense brightness, eyes glued and feeling the pain until she felt like He wanted her to look away. Blinking and blinded, tears running in pain, again she heard Yeshua speak and ask, *"What do you see, Joy?"*

Her response? "All I see is the sun."

Now, I feel like I need to add a "Don't try this at home" clause right here. We've all been told by parents and teachers that looking into the sun is dangerous, and they're probably right. Looking into the sun certainly isn't for everyone (or anyone, maybe). But for Joy, she had an extremely unique encounter with Yeshua. In an instant she realized the message He wanted to speak into her circumstances. If she fixed her eyes on the Son—on Yeshua—it was going to burn. It was going to purify. It was going to be intense, it was going to burn off the dross in her life.[14]

---

13. James 1:22-25
14. Isaiah 1:25-27

*But with eyes fixed on Him, she would see Him in
everything.*

She would only see glory and holiness, with no shadow of
darkness. She wouldn't see her shame or her failures or her
shortcomings in the light of Yeshua's presence. She would
walk in the truth that she has become the righteousness of
Elohim in Yeshua Messiah.[15]

*She would walk illuminated by the glory of His presence
as she offered herself to be purified in holiness.*

I'm not endorsing that you should go out and stare at
the sun like Joy did, but I hope her testimony leaves just as
powerful of an impact on your heart as if you did. I know it did
for me. Holiness transcends every aspect of life, changing how
we view the world and how we interact with it.

*Walking in holiness is a place of glory, a dazzling
brightness of Adonai's presence on earth that I never
want to leave.*

When Adonai says you're forgiven, He means it. When He
says you are chosen, He isn't kidding around. When He labels
you as holy, He's serious.

*When He calls you to be holy, He has faith that you can
achieve it through His power.[16]*

---

15. 2 Corinthians 5:21
16. Leviticus 11:45

1.   Look up each verse footnoted in this chapter. Write the
       ones that spoke to your heart below.

2.   Write down three things that have clouded your view from
       seeing holiness all around you.

3.   Write down three things that have helped illuminate your
       view to see holiness all around you.

4.   Take a look again at Luke 15:11-32. How do you relate to
       the story of the prodigal son? Be specific.

5. What are some pig pits (un-kosher situations) in your life that you need to leave behind?

6. Are you holding onto any giants of guilt so that you are unable to slip your arms into the robes of royalty Adonai is offering you? List them below. Then, write out a prayer asking Adonai to help you slay these giants once and for all in order to enter into all the holiness He desires for you.

7. Read Psalm 15. What aspects of holiness does Adonai desire in the people who dwell with Him?

8. How do you rate yourself when compared to these qualities? What are some areas you need to work on, and what choices will you make to be intentional in cultivating them?

9. Share one recent situation that could have been a sinkhole in your life, but instead you chose to use it as a launching pad to pursue more holiness.

10. Share a testimony of a time when you felt the conviction of the Holy Spirit. How does knowing that Elohim goes with you change your choices on the places you go?

11. Joy's testimony about the sun was so powerful in my life, and I hope it was powerful for you, too. What would life look like if you kept your eyes fixed on Yeshua? How might it help you pursue holiness? How might it change your perspective on things?

12. Many times, people assume holiness is a burden or a list of restrictions (can't go to this movie, can't go out with certain friends, can't read that book), but how is holiness a place of glory, instead?

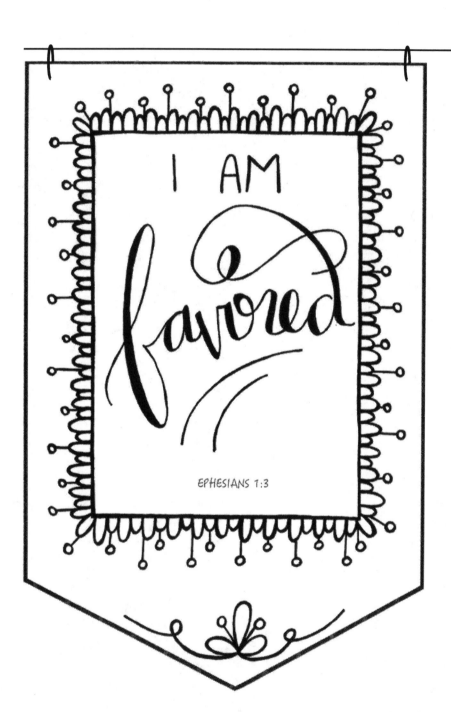

CHAPTER TWELVE

You Are Favored

Dear Favored You,

Open wide to receive all Adonai has to pour into your cupped hands.

This good, good Father that we serve, He has storehouses of goodness with your name on them. He has a good measure, pressed down, shaken together, and running over, ready to be given to you.[1] His heart is bursting with joy over you, bursting to show you the depths of His love.

Your expectations are about to be blown out of the water.

For generations, religion has taught us to create a box for Adonai, as if these were the only perimeters He frequented. If we were to open up this cardboard carton, we'd see a list of what our actions should be in order to merit His responses, an analytical review of how Elohim interacts with His children. We believe if we do *abc*, He'll respond with *xyz*. If we stay in this box, we know what He'll do.

Here's the truth: Adonai has never allowed Himself to be boxed in.

Regardless of the pressures and demands in your life, He has it in His heart to prosper you, not to bring you down

---

1.   Luke 6:38

in harm.[2] He's not sitting on His throne on high with His fist clenched around a javelin, eager to strike you down at your first offense. He's not tight-lipped, or reluctant to speak His blessing until you've gotten every area of your life straightened out. His idea of love isn't to just check in with you from time to time, tossing a few provisions your way just to keep you sustained. His goal is not to keep you at the bottom of the food chain, trampled upon by other's successes.

He wants to make you the head, not the tail, to place you above, not beneath.[3]

Adonai is not here to make your life miserable, to pound you with the hailstones of heaven, or to beat you to the ground. He's not here to make things too difficult to bear, to take away all your joy. If only we trusted His heart, we'd see the enormous depth of His love. We'd see Him chasing and choosing us as His chief delight.

He's here to build you up, to root you deep, to overflow you with gratitude.[4]

The fear of Elohim is not a shrinking terror of His wrath, but an awe of His great holiness. He doesn't want fear to separate you from Him, but instead, to draw you nearer. He wants you to approach Him with freedom and confidence,[5] without shackles of confining religious lists to merit His favor, and without fear of being pummeled.

He wants you to see the world through His eyes of delight and love.

Every day, every breath, every moment is a gift from His heart to yours, a glorious romance, a dance of delight. You

2.   Jeremiah 29:11
3.   Deuteronomy 28:13
4.   Colossians 2:7
5.   Ephesians 3:12

can hear the gift in the songbird's warble, you can see it in the sunset-streaked sky, you can feel it with hands cupping your favorite latte. You can smell it in fresh laundry, you can taste it around the dinner table, you can touch it in the hug of a friend.

Every day is a declaration that you are here for abundant life and blessing.[6]

When you live knowing you are favored, life becomes a treasure hunt of looking for these little gifts, knowing that you come preferred and recommended by the Almighty. It's not a question of *if* He shows up, it's just a matter of *when*. It's living in the confidence of the expressions of His love. You're not a second thought or one more name on His list.

You are the one His heart relentlessly seeks.

Through Him, you have obtained an inheritance among the greats, a solemn vow that He will work all things according to the counsel of His good and perfect will.[7] You have been blessed with every spiritual blessing in Yeshua.[8] Read that again. *Every blessing.* Not just some blessing, not even an equal portion that you need to split with your neighbor.

All of the blessings. Every last drop. Not one blessing left behind.

Maybe you've felt behind before. I know in moments of self-centeredness, I have. One week in particular stands out to me. I was feeling discouraged, like I'm always pouring out into others but rarely do people take the time to listen to the Holy Spirit and pour into me. Others don't realize that even the encouragers need encouragement. They assume that since we

6.   John 10:10
7.   Ephesians 1:11
8.   Ephesians 1:3

speak abundant life over others, our own lives are hunky-dory. They think we have no need for words of life spoken into us, no need of a refill of our joy tanks.

It's true that we shouldn't look to others to supply our joy, but sometimes it's nice to know we're appreciated.

At the end of that week, I went to my mailbox and found an out-of-the-blue letter waiting there from my sweet friend Cassie. During a week that held no personal mail up to that point, holding the letter itself was a special treat to my letter-loving heart. The thick, lined envelope told me that it wasn't a cheap "Hi, how's life?" note. It told me that it wasn't part of a mass "just keeping up on my correspondence" dutiful epistle. I broke the floral sticker seal to pull out a beautiful card, and goose bumps tingled up my arms.

It was like Adonai gave Cassie a vision about every single place in which I needed encouragement.

She listened to the Holy Spirit and wrote encouragements she didn't even know I needed to hear. I was totally blown away by Elohim's faithfulness. Right there, sitting in my car next to my mailbox, Adonai revealed to me how favored I was. To the outsider, it may just look like all I had received was a nice letter. End of story. Truly, it was only the beginning. Such a simple moment, yet so significantly big. It was one letter, to one woman, in one mailbox, on one street, in one community, in one city, in one state, in one nation, on one continent, in one hemisphere, on one planet, in one universe...and Elohim showed up.

If you trail the story, it leaves you in awe of being chosen. Of knowing you are favored. Of each one of us being preferred to the heart of Elohim.

Adonai is extravagant and artful and merciful—and maybe a little crazy, too—in His display of favor towards you. He meets you in the little details, again crossing infinite heaven with finite humanity. The Elohim who spins galaxies in His Hand is the same One Who places that $5 bill you forgot about in your coat pocket right when you need the extra cash. He's the One Who places the perfect sweater you've been looking for on the clearance rack. He's the One Who clears traffic when you're running late and the One Who prompts your friend to put flowers on your desk. Favor means you are preferred, the girl His heart is chasing after. Maybe that's hard to wrap your mind around...maybe it was hard for Mary, too.[9]

She was a betrothed teenager on the cusp of change, thrown into a situation that was altogether terrifying, and yet she's called favored.

Imagine for a moment being in Mary's place. Legally married to a man she's not living with, she's waiting for him to claim her as his wife. She may not have even known much about Joseph. Perhaps it was a match her parents arranged and she trusted their judgement. What would her betrothed say about her carrying a child not his own? What would her family say, thinking she had an unknown child out of wedlock? What would her community say as the gossip filtered through town? Yet, in the middle of an angel's story and her life looking like a scandal for the sake of Heaven coming to earth, Mary is called favored.[10] She's chosen. She is the preferred one, the one into whom Adonai wanted to implant the seed of His Son.

Mary receives this favor. She knows she is chosen for this moment.

Mary, the small-town girl, knows how to trail this moment into perspective. In the midst of the flashing glory of an angel speaking destiny over her, she realizes she's just one girl, in

9.   Luke 1:26-56
10.   Luke 1:28

one home, in one community, in one town, in one tribe, in one nation, on one continent, in one hemisphere, on one planet, in one universe...

...and Elohim shows up.

More than that, He shows up in the worship of two women experiencing the favor of Adonai, simultaneously carrying sons in their wombs that contradict natural possibility because they are preferred among women for His redemptive plan. His favor upon both Mary and Elizabeth moves them to some of the most poetic praise in the Gospel story. His Spirit upon them turns each tongue into that of a prophetess, declaring Adonai's plan of salvation to the world. Elizabeth speaks encouragement and blessing over a trembling girl, and Mary's gut response to all this is to recall Scriptures she had saved in her heart, weaving them into a new song.

What is your response when Elohim shows up?

Is your response praise? Prayer? The overflowing of Scripture promises from your heart? Do you pass by these moments, or do you create a space of grateful reflection? Mary treasures this place of being favored, keeping each precious memory in a special place in her heart.[11] She knows the road won't be easy. Being favored to mother the Son of Elohim was a job for which she certainly didn't feel qualified. She knew there'd be criticism and the extreme weight of feeling like the salvation of the world rests on her parenting. Yet, she doesn't let the pain and heartache and pressures snuff out the joy of being chosen. It's as if she's gathering these moments like seashells along the beach, placing each one carefully in a jar as a memorial and testament of this journey of favor.

---

11.   Luke 2:19

*She could scoop up a jar of ocean water blessing, not
even realizing that Adonai wants to give her the whole
ocean of favor.*

Maybe you've collected your jar filled with ocean liquid, too.
Maybe you've sealed it and placed it on your shelf, thinking
that's all the favor that has been allotted for your lifetime. It's a
memorial of just a moment, just a season, one for the books.
Maybe you're in the trenches now and this place doesn't feel
like there could possibly be favor in the mud-lined holes. You
long for that moment of delight again.

*You're favored even here—chosen for the hard-trench
moments to bring out your gold.*

Oh yes, even here you are favored. He has chosen to
refine you, to pan through the silt to reveal the most sparkling
glimmers of character and perseverance in you. And that jar
of ocean water favor, sitting on your shelf? It's quaking and
slipping towards the edge, ready to topple over and spill fresh
favor anew upon your head.

*He wants to blow your little sealed jars of expectations out
of the water and give you the entire ocean instead.*

His heart in favoring you isn't just for your sake alone.
It brings great joy to Him, to watch in delight as you gather
His love notes along the journey. He wants your heart to sing
as loudly as His does. The smile spreading across your face
when you discover His favor matches the smile on His face
when He gives it.

*So open wide your cupped hands, girl, with no reserves
or lists or expectations, and watch the ocean of Adonai's
blessing cascade into your life in overflowing waterfalls.*

1. Look up each verse footnoted in this chapter. Write the
ones that spoke to your heart below.

2. Have you grown up with religious expectations of how
Elohim interacts with His children? How has this affected
your relationship with Him?

3. When you think of Elohim, what is the first thing that comes to your mind?

4. A dear friend of mine once painted this word picture: You enter into a great throne room, and at the opposite end sits Adonai. You know that you just messed up, and you see Him sitting there with cold disappointment in His eyes and a gavel in His hand. Do you feel like approaching Him in that moment? Now picture the same scenario, except Adonai—with the heart of a loving Father—meets you halfway down the long hall. He picks you up and holds you close to His heartbeat. He explains how He's disappointed, but His love doesn't change. There will be consequences, but you will always be His beloved one. How does your view of Adonai change your response? How does it change your relationship? Which view have you had?

5. In what areas do you want a deeper understanding of Adonai's heart for you? Write out a prayer below, and know that He will reveal greater measures!

6. Share what the "fear of Elohim" means to you.

7. Reread your answer to the previous question. Is this a healthy fear? Does it propel you deeper into Adonai, or cause a greater division from Him? What needs to change in order for you to pursue more of Him?

8. Every little thing that comes into your day is a gift from Adonai's heart to yours. Today, take a special note of His love song over you—when you're given a great parking spot, when you see a flower blooming in the garden, when a butterfly flutters by your window. Record His gifts to you today:

9. Ephesians 1:3 says that you have been blessed with *every spiritual blessing*. How does this equip you? How does it cause you to live in favor?

10. In this chapter, I shared how Cassie's letter to me was a display of Adonai's favor to my heart. How does "trailing the story" of Elohim's favor give you greater perspective on how committed He is to showing up in your life? Try it yourself. Think of one situation this week where you experienced His favor, and trail it back to Adonai!

11. Mary's response to favor was worship and prophecy, even in the middle of uncertainty. How do you respond to Adonai's favor in the hard seasons of life?

12. Read Luke 2:19 again. How do you treasure Adonai's favor in your heart?

CHAPTER THIRTEEN

You Are Free

Dear Free You,

I pray you dance like no one is watching.

Arms flailing, feet stomping, heart pounding in praise. The kind of dance where the Holy Spirit totally takes over and you are immersed into a waterfall of Adonai's presence. The kind of response to glory that leaves your soul tingling in wonder. Dancing with all your heart, all your soul- all your being- in an epic display of worship and gratitude.

I pray you never stop. Ever.

I pray your worship brings Heaven down to earth, and that praise refreshes everyone who comes in contact with you. I pray you are refreshed as you drink deep from Yeshua's well of living water, bubbling over with joy.[1] I pray you splash droplets of this celebration onto everyone you meet as you jump into His delight with both feet.

You have this freedom.

You have freedom and permission to be the beautiful creation Elohim created you to be, filled with His character and endowed with special uniqueness. You have the freedom

---

1. Isaiah 12:3

to worship, to praise, to pray. You have the freedom to share, the freedom to receive. You have the freedom to walk in the way of love, following the footsteps of Yeshua where He leads.[2]

You have the freedom to meet with the Creator in the ways that are most meaningful to your heart.

Maybe you've grown up being taught that worship can only look a certain way, that prayer can only follow certain words, that praise must be in a certain order. Maybe you've been afraid, or scared, or ashamed to do anything differently. Maybe your heart is longing to worship in the fullness of Spirit and truth, but you're not sure how.[3] Maybe the tugging of the Holy Spirit on your heart shakes things up and breaks the mold, asking you to go a way that's not popular.

I'll let you in on an unpopular secret. My most raw moments of prayer and intensity of heart are often revealed sitting on the bathroom floor.

For years, it was my ideal prayer space. Lock the door and no one will ever question where you are, while people will pound on your bedroom door no matter what signs you tape as a warning. I could bawl my eyes out with the fan on and no one would hear. I could stifle sobs while the shower water ran in the background and no one would guess twice. I could sit there on the floor with worship music in my earbuds and pleading prayers forming on trembling lips. Those few squares of linoleum behind that bathroom door were my sacred space, my hollowed ground, my battlefield lines.

Until I realized praying in the bathroom was forbidden by rabbinical law.

---

2.   Ephesians 5:2
3.   John 4:23

So, I stopped. I stopped worshipping and praying warrior prayers in the bathroom...and as life happens, I stopped praying them anywhere else. In a busy house, there wasn't privacy afforded anywhere else like the seclusion of the bathroom to enter into intense intercession. There were days I would catch myself beginning a prayer while doing my makeup or cleaning my shower, and would promptly squelch it with a twinge of guilt when I realized what I was doing.

I allowed others to dictate my heart, rather than the Spirit.

Don't get me wrong, the rabbis and sages have wisdom to share, knowledge that I eagerly drink up. There is so much they offer that I gratefully walk in, but if the Holy Spirit is prodding me in a different way, I need to be one who responds to Adonai before men. It's not a choice I take lightly, it's not a quick decision I put little thought to. It involves a lot of prayer, a lot of counsel, a lot of asking for confirmation to do so.

But, where the Spirit of Adonai is, there is freedom.[4]

This same Spirit that is like the wind, rushing hither and thither, cannot be contained within a box of religious principles.[5] Oh, the Spirit can be moving among man's well-meaning rules and regulations, but it cannot be limited to just that. It flows and bends, it adapts to different courses and moves around obstacles. It cannot be pinned down to stay down. It is free. Free to move, free to express, free to pursue the promptings of Adonai.

As a reflection of the Master's glory, I am free to bend with the moving of the Spirit.

This isn't a license for rebellion, for taking a big spoon and stirring the pot of religious regulations until everything is

---

4.   2 Corinthians 3:17-18
5.   John 3:8

jumbled. This isn't about bucking the system and blazing your own lonely trail. It's not about being divisive or causing discord.

It's simply about listening to the still small voice of the Spirit, and having the courage to follow His leading.[6]

It's a tightrope balance, isn't it? Torah and Yeshua, law and spirit, regulations and freedom. The one needs the other, but knowing how to balance the ratio is difficult. So many people struggle on this tightrope. So many people fall. Yet, where we are called—aligning with Scripture—we must go with beautiful grace, standing firm in the freedom we've been given.[7]

Walking free in the Spirit is beautiful, but it is also uncomfortable.

I like following religious rules. They give structure to my otherwise color-outside-the-lines kind of life. While my heart craves spontaneity, regulations bring me back to reality. They bring richness and meaning, they pull me deeper into Yeshua. They keep my dreams based in reality.

I don't like to break them.

Nevertheless, in the above story, my soul began to feel a little wilted from my restrained prayer. Without water, a plant can't grow, and without prayer, a soul can't develop. Yet, one day in the bathroom my tired soul realized: I am free from the laws that bring sin, and I am free from the laws that bring death.[8] I am free from the man-made laws that weigh down my soul when the Spirit asks me to soar instead. I have been given grace. I have been given freedom to couple all knowledge with the interpretation of the Spirit, letting Him direct the way for my heart.

6.   1 Kings 19:12
7.   Galatians 5:1
8.   Romans 8:2

So right there in the bathroom, I began with warrior praise again.

That day, I thought of King David, the man after Elohim's own heart, a man in touch with the Holy Spirit, a man in passionate pursuit for Adonai's glory.[9] I thought of how he was able to dance with all his might in the sight of Adonai and all the nation of Israel, wearing but a linen ephod.[10] The mighty king of Israel humbled himself to the Spirit's prompting, stripping off all pretenses, and he danced with all of his soul. His wife was mortified at his display of peasant-like behavior, and she pointed out the scandal of it all. How unpopular and unpolitical an action, and how bold of a risk it was. How susceptible he made himself to rumors and gossip.

David didn't see the people. He only saw Adonai and the pathway on which He was leading.

David didn't become discouraged by his wife's politically correct outburst. He had laser-focused vision on pursuing Adonai in every moment. He was committed to continuing worshipping before Adonai, he was willing to become even more undignified and humbled in his pursuit of listening to the voice of Elohim. He was willing to lay it all on the line—with the entire royal court thinking he was wrong—in pursuit of freedom to follow wherever the Spirit led.

If David could do this, I too could put my shame and pride and religious pressures aside to do the same. To worship in Spirit and in truth.

I'm not saying heart-cry prayers in the bathroom is for everyone, but for me it's one area where the Spirit is leading me to be free. I'm not saying it's right or wrong, or whether or

9.   Acts 13:22
10.   2 Samuel 6:14

not I'll always storm Heaven's gates sitting on those linoleum squares.

But today this is where the Spirit of Adonai is, and it is where I find freedom for my soul.

I don't know what that thing is for you, the one area you're afraid to be free and pursue the Spirit's prompting. Maybe it's raising your hands in surrendered worship while the rest of the congregation has their arms glued to their sides. Maybe it's praying over someone in a room of friends who might think you're weird for doing so. Maybe it's writing down the vision Adonai gives you on a Shabbat morning. Maybe it's eating at an uncertified Kosher restaurant because someone you know is desperate to share their heavy heart with you over lunch. (Side note: *Salad.* There is always salad. In all serious gratitude: *Baruch atah Adonai, Eloheinu Melech Ha'Olam borei pri ha-adamah!*[11])

The point is not to buck the system. The point is to be flexible to the Spirit's leading.

The day I began to pour out my heart in prayer in the bathroom again, I felt the Spirit of Adonai upon me. I felt His delight, I felt the freedom. I laughed and cried and danced in celebration. I reclaimed the intimacy of sharing my soul with Him, of letting Him have His perfect way in me. I put on worship music and allowed myself to dance while brushing my teeth, I allowed myself to stop from time to time with hands raised and declare His promises.

There is a law, but it is a law of liberty.[12]

---

11. "Blessed are You, Lord our God, King of the universe, Who creates the fruit of the earth."
12. James 1:25

I pray that every aspect of your life is drenched in the Spirit, that you are so in tune to His leading that you have the boldness and courage to press into the things Adonai is speaking to your heart. I pray you have ears that understand His still small voice, that you act upon it and that you surrender to it. I pray you make choices in humility, that you seek after wisdom. I pray you are saturated in grace, and that you extend that grace to others.

I pray you embrace this freedom with a gentle touch, with a balance of Torah's structure and Yeshua's heart.

1.   Look up each verse footnoted in this chapter. Write the
      ones that spoke to your heart below.

2.   What does freedom in your relationship with Yeshua
      mean to you? What does it look like? How does your
      worship look with this in mind?

3. In what ways are you free to express the unique personality and giftings He has given you?

4. Think of your ideal, most meaningful way of experiencing Adonai's presence. Where does it take place, and when? How do you feel? What does it look like?

5. I shared in this chapter how I had stopped praying in the bathroom because doing so was against rabbinic law. Has there ever been a situation where you stopped pursuing Adonai because you felt like it was wrong by others' standards to do so?

_____
_____
_____
_____
_____
_____
_____
_____
_____
_____
_____
_____
_____

6. Read 2 Corinthians 3:17-18. What does this passage mean to you? How do you interpret verse 17, and in what ways could it apply to your answer above?

_____
_____
_____
_____
_____
_____
_____
_____
_____
_____
_____

7. Share one area of your life where you feel like you have a good balance of Spirit and Law, Torah and Yeshua.

8. In what ways do you enjoy religious regulations? How are they beneficial to you?

9. David took a risk when he followed the Spirit's leading and danced with all his might. Have you ever taken a risk in following the Spirit's leading in your life? Share below.

10. We all have at least one area where we're afraid to be free. What is that one area for you? It is critical to remember that we're not out to start a rebellion. Our heart is not to buck the system or chart our own paths. How will you be flexible to the Spirit's touch in this area, as well as handle religious regulations with grace?

11. How do you feel when you live in touch with the Holy Spirit and encounter the freedom of Adonai? List the emotions below, and share a time when you've experienced this.

12. I closed this chapter with a prayer that I believe sums up living in the Spirit. You might want to make it your mission statement for living a Spirit-filled life. Write it on a sticky note and use it as a bookmark in your Bible: *I embrace freedom in the Spirit with a gentle touch, with a balance of Torah's structure and Yeshua's heart.*

I AM

alive

ROMANS 6:11

CHAPTER FOURTEEN

You Are Alive

Dear Alive You,

Your life is a celebration of Elohim's glory.

You're not a mistake, an accident, or an overlooked detail. You were made with intention, with purpose, with glorious plans that would take your breath away if you knew them in full.

In Yeshua, you are a new creation, with all your old past put away.[1]

You carry no shame as a daughter redeemed by Yeshua. This new redeemed you, it's being renewed in the knowledge of the One Who created you.[2] You are flourishing, blossoming, fruitful and green olive tree, planted in the house of Elohim.[3]

An olive tree doesn't try to move elsewhere. It sinks its roots deep right where it is planted.

In an instant, while reading Psalm 52:8 about the olive tree, I'm transported to the heart of the heartland, the pulse of Jerusalem: *Har HaBayit*,[4] the Temple Mount. I see the silver-green olive trees, their kinky and gnarly branches twisted

---

1.   2 Corinthians 5:17
2.   Colossians 3:9-10
3.   Psalm 52:8
4.   Literally "Mountain of the House" in Hebrew

upwards with a story to tell. In the midst of political unrest and faced with desecration, they know exactly who they are and don't doubt the role they play. They are not detained from their purpose, but rather established. Waiting for the Temple to exist in their midst, they patiently stay rooted and expectant for that great day. They let down a harvest of fruit, olives fat and nourishing, as if to say, "No matter how long it takes, even now we will be preparing the oil to light the menorah."

They live a life of thankfulness and holy joy. They are fruitful, even when circumstances aren't perfect.

I smile as I think of you doing the same. I wonder how your life of thankfulness and holy joy will look. I can imagine the bold and glorious things you will do, living to the heartbeat of Elohim, carrying the character of Yeshua. I think of the fruits of the Spirit you will bear right here in the season you are in, regardless of the circumstances.

You have been made alive, together with Messiah.[5]

Heart beating, soul singing, passionately bursting in praise. Every fiber fused in faith, every cell programmed to celebrate. This is what new life looks like: dying to sin and having Yeshua live within.[6] You are a living stone in Elohim's house,[7] anchored on top of the cornerstone of Messiah.[8] It's a picture that the Temple of Adonai is not just a brick and mortar building. No, it's alive and breathing. It has the Spirit pouring in and through our living souls. The *Beit HaMikdash*[9] is built with every one of us, a collective with no one left behind.

---

5.   Ephesians 2:5
6.   Galatians 2:20
7.   1 Peter 2:5
8.   Matthew 21:42
9.   "The Sanctified House," the Temple

We are dead to the power of sin, and alive in the Spirit of Elohim.[10]

What if you lived like you were alive? It may seem like a silly question, but in all seriousness, many people go through the motions of *living* without actually being *alive*. They wake up, do their jobs, grab a quick bite to eat on the way to meetings, then hit the bed only to do it all over again. It's a rat-race life that drains both energy and inspiration. I'm sure you know several people like this. Maybe you're even one of them. For such people, life isn't an intentional choice, it's just a flow-with-the-crowd motion, letting culture and superiors make choices for them.

Do you want to simply live, or do you want to be fully alive?

What if you woke up to a life with purpose and lived fully alive in the Spirit of Elohim? Instead of surviving, what if you chose to thrive? Instead of hiding, what would you find in His light? Instead of being passive, what if you lived with passion? Instead of being reactive, how would you be proactive?

Life is a gift and every moment is slipping away until the clock runs out.

I'll never forget the 4:30 a.m. text I received exactly two years ago as I write this, asking if I heard about what happened to my childhood best friend. As a girl, she was filled with life and chasing after the next big thing. She was a dreamer who fueled the dreams of others, one of the most jealously loyal people you'd ever meet. I knew she always had my back, but as life went on and different circumstances arose, we lost touch as we entered our teens.

---

10. Romans 6:11

Next thing I know, I receive a text saying that this beautifully created twenty-three year old committed suicide.

Her funeral was one of the hardest events of my life. I had never lost someone I was so close to—who I had loved so dearly—ever before. The entire circumstance was a crushing weight so heavy to bear, knowing all the truth and hope that was available to her and yet she couldn't see it. Bits and pieces of the chapters of her life I had missed began to filter in. Her thirst for adventure led her down dark roads we never would have dreamed of as girls. Her pursuit of acceptance led to despair. The monotony of simply living dragged her to a place she could no longer endure.

She struggled to accept the concept that she could be fully alive in Yeshua.

Her story is a horrific reminder that we were created for more than living just to live. Without purpose, she drifted. The enemy spoke lies to her lonely heart, and she received them. Her choice didn't simply destroy her life, but it totally altered the lives of her family, her siblings, her friends. She knew Yeshua's love was there, but instead, she chased after other things that could never satisfy her need.

Her life may be over, but I am determined that the enemy won't have the last word.

His intent may be destruction, but that won't be the last chapter. I still believe Adonai will use her story, perhaps even here in these pages. Maybe you've been coasting along on neutral, with no one at the steering wheel. Maybe your life feels devoid of something, like a piece is missing but you're not sure what. Maybe you're discouraged with your life. Maybe you're yearning for something more meaningful than your own rat-race of classes and work and social political correctness.

You can choose to live fully alive.

As I sat there at her funeral with a grieving soul, I vowed to carry the torch she had dropped. I would know my identity, and I would be confident in it. I wouldn't just live, I would be alive. I wouldn't follow the crowd, I'd be attentive to march to Adonai's drumbeat. I'd be in touch with the giftings and passions He has given me, and I'd use them to impact others. I wouldn't seek my own acceptance, I'd seek to proclaim His glory.

I'd see tulips every spring as a reminder of life.

I remember the dozens of tulip bulbs she planted one spring, totally unaware of what colors they were. We laughed months later at the random patterns they made. And now, I'll never view a tulip the same way. There is a tender ache in my soul, because the story of a tulip's growth is so relevant to our lives, and could have drastically changed hers had she stopped to meditate on it.

Unless a bulb goes through a dark, cold season, it won't bloom.

No matter what time of darkness you feel, spring blooms are certainly coming. You could view the heaviness of soil over you as suffocating, or you could view it as life-producing. You may feel that this season of winter may never end, that no good could ever come from the pain.

Yet tulips live to push on through the darkness, up into the light because they know that Elohim is alive.

How would you live if you lived like Elohim is alive? Like you *truly* believed it with every fiber of your being, like your whole existence hinged on it? How would your prayers be if you truly believed He was listening? How would you give if you truly believed He would provide? How would your world change if religion changed to relationship, if life became a partnership?

It would change everything.

I want to live in the fullness of Adonai through the power of Yeshua. We have been raised with Yeshua, and our hearts are set on things above.[11] He has made known the ways of life, filling us with joy in His presence.[12] Living in those promises, I'd be confident every time I rose from kneeling in intercession. I'd stand in the face of danger unafraid. I'd take the risk and stake it all on faith because I know He won't let me down if I am following after His heart.

Life isn't about playing it safe, it's about leaving it all on the field.

So what is it, friend? What are those moments when you feel closest to His heartbeat, when you feel your own heart flutter wildly with joy? What are those dreams He has placed in your soul that you've been smothering with a blanket of security and safety?

It's time to throw caution to the wind, and to step out with wings to soar.

It's time to live your life with thankfulness and holy joy. To live fully alive, thriving passionately in pursuit of Yeshua's heart. Your wild adventure of faith begins right here, right now, today. Your unique journey is tailor-made, a romance from Elohim's heart to yours.

It's an adventure written by Him where values and vision align.

---

11. Colossians 3:1
12. Acts 2:28

Without vision, the people perish,[13] and your values set your vision. Your values are those things you just can't live without, that you can't stop yourself from doing. They're those concepts that are dear to your heart, the ones that motivate you and keep you driven. I used to think values were only faith-related, but they're so much more. It's not just the value of fairness, of life, of truth. It's values of organization, of health, of encouragement, of relationships. It's the value of time alone to process for the introvert, and the value of creativity for the artist.

Our values act as a map for our vision, as signposts leading to what means the most to us and where our calling lies.

Knowing what we value is like a neon sign, telling us what makes us feel fully alive. Your values will be as unique as you are, and when you're living in tune with them, you'll discover those beautiful callings for which Elohim has created you.

So what core values are near and dear to your heart?

Dig deep to discover them, and pray over what direction they may be leading you. Take hold of your steering wheel, and make your own choices instead of sitting back and allowing culture to make them for you. This is your time to shine, to thrive, to passionately come alive.

Abide in Yeshua's love, and live fully and fruitfully alive.[14]

---

13. Proverbs 29:18
14. John 15:5

1. Look up each verse footnoted in this chapter. Write the ones that spoke to your heart below.

2. What does redemption mean to you? Feel free to use additional Scripture verses to explain.

3. How does the story of the olive trees speak to you? How does it change your perspective on fruitfulness and joy?

4. In what ways have you simply lived without being fully alive? What would your life look like if you chose to radiate thankfulness and holy joy in Yeshua? What is preventing you from living alive in this place?

5. In this chapter, I shared the hard story of my childhood best friend who gave up on life. Do you know of a similar situation? What did you learn about the life Adonai wants you to have through it?

6. Tulips remind me every year of Adonai's faithfulness and that we were created to push through the dark seasons into new life. Do you have a similar reminder? If so, share below. If not, what could be your physical reminder to keep pushing through the dirt in order to grow and bloom?

7. How would you live if you truly believed Adonai is alive? How would it change your prayers, your worship, your relationship with others? What confidence would you receive, and what would it cause you to do?

8. Life isn't about playing it safe. In what ways have you been playing it safe, and how are you going to step out in faith, instead?

9. Think of the values that are important to you. If you need help, do an internet search on "core values" and look at several example lists. Pray about it, and write the values that are important to you.

10. Your values and vision should be aligned. For example, if you value health, you're not going to feel fulfilled working at a fast food restaurant. However, you may feel fulfilled as a personal chef for an elderly couple who are unable to cook for themselves. Another example would be, if you value creativity, you won't feel fulfilled doing paperwork all day. In that case, you might feel fulfilled teaching art or being an entrepreneur instead. Keep praying over your values and how they play into Elohim's vision for you. Brainstorm your ideas below.

11. Read John 10:10. What does abundant life in Yeshua mean to you? How will you live out this principle?

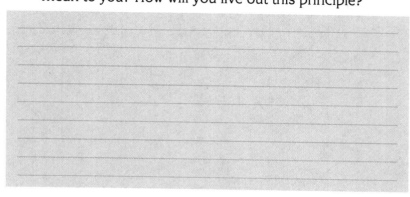

CONCLUSION

This Is Your Identity

I hope every page of this book has spoken truth into your soul, and empowered you to become all Adonai has created you to be. It's been quite the journey, hasn't it? I think we could all breathe out a happy sigh of relief, of release, of joy. It would be easy to leave all these Heavenly-orchestrated moments on the pages, place this book on your shelf, and move on to the next thing life brings.

But there's one more letter left, my friend.

Perhaps this is the most important letter of this entire book, because it's *your* letter. It's the letter you will write to yourself, a declaration of identity, of who you are in Yeshua and of the promises He speaks over you.

This is your identity statement.

I didn't ask you tough questions at the end of each chapter for no reason. Through the process of answering them, you've been discovering more about yourself, about what makes you soar, about what your testimony and story have been. You've written out Scripture passages where Adonai has spoken to you and taught you more about Himself through them.

You've been finding your identity in Yeshua.

You've been discovering who you are in Him, and who Adonai has created you to be. You've been discovering your passions and talents, your values and your calling. You might not feel like you have all the pieces yet, but let me assure you, they will come.

Wait on Adonai, and He will come.

Don't rush this process. Take your time, and take it slowly. Saturate every word of your identity statement in prayer, and be still enough to hear His heartbeat for you. There are no wrong words, and no two identity statements will look the same. It can be short and sweet, or long and deep.

This is a declaration to your soul, a reminder of who you are—who you will always be—in Yeshua's love.

1. This entire book has really been on the identity Adonai speaks over you in Scripture, so naturally this is the very first place we need to look to start building our identity statements. At the end of every chapter, I've asked you to look up all the Scripture references and to copy out the ones that have meant something special to your heart. Look back at all the ones you've written down. Is there a theme? A certain promise Adonai speaks over you that means something special in your soul? Think back over any Scripture verses that have been your favorites over the years. See if your name has a Scripture reference attached to it. Ask Adonai to reveal more of His heart for you through these passages.

2. As you've answered all the questions at the end of every chapter, you've been discovering more about yourself and who Adonai has created you to be. You've been creating a legacy and a written testimony of the work Yeshua is doing in your soul. Go ahead and flip through all your answers, re-read them and discover any themes. I've listed a few questions below to help jumpstart discovering more of your identity. I've given the chapter and question reference where you've already written down these answers, but I've reworded the questions here in order to help you be specific and to prompt additional thoughts. Flip back through your answers and allow the Holy Spirit to guide you.

    You Are Forgiven: Question 9. What defines you in Yeshua?

    You Are Beautiful: Question 10. What legacy do you want to create? How will your choices today enable you to achieve this legacy?

You Are Chosen: Question 6. What ways are you most available and effective for the Kingdom?

You Are Not Alone: Question 7. How can you impact your community? What community has Adonai given you?

You Are Gifted: Question 3. What do other people say your talents are? What are some positive things people always say about you?

You Are Equipped: Question 2. What talents do you have that have been constant throughout your life?

You Are An Overcomer: Question 7. What do your first, middle, and last names mean? How can they be put together to declare a deeper meaning and purpose for your life? Are you named after anyone, and are there any character traits from that person's life that you carry as well?

You Are Royalty: Question 6. What labels does Yeshua write on your soul?

You Are Healed: Question 10. Are you a quitter or a victor? How does that empower you?

You Are Beloved: Question 3. How would your life look if you were focused on Yeshua? What would your worship look like?

You Are Holy: Question 8. What qualities are you cultivating in your life?

You Are Favored: Question 9. What Spiritual blessings do you have? What are your Spiritual gifts?

You Are Free: Question 3. How do you express the unique personality Adonai has given you? In what ways do you walk in freedom to express it?

You Are Alive: Question 10. What are your values and vision? How do they align? In what ways do they create a purpose where you feel fulfilled and fully alive?

3. We all need to be firm in our identity in Yeshua. We all need to know who we were created to be, and we long for affirmation in those areas. Consider playing the "edification game" with a group of friends/family. The rules are simple: one person is chosen, and everyone else in the circle speaks edification and appreciation over that person. While others are speaking about you, you're not allowed to speak, but instead, only absorb and accept the words of life being spoken over you (it helps to record the audio on your phone!). It's so beautiful when others are in tune with the Holy Spirit that they speak prophetic words over you, as well. Pay attention to patterns and words that resonate with your soul. Perhaps someone will say something about your smile, or about how much they appreciate the way you include others. The game is played until every person has had a turn being chosen to receive edification. Write some of the key words or phrases spoken over you below:

4.   Adonai has placed dreams deep within each one of us, and we need to call them out and pursue them with purpose. It's time to dream big, my friend! What is that big, crazy dream that has lingered in your heart all your life? Think back to your childhood. What were some of your dreams? Do those dreams still reoccur in your heart today? How could these be an indication of your calling? If you had no limitations, if you had no obstacles, what would you do for the sake of the Kingdom? It can be scary giving voice to those secret dreams you've held silent in your heart for so long, but it's time to give them wings to soar!

5.   Looking back at all the answers you've given on these pages, try to collect them into specific concepts. Format concepts to answer questions, such as:

What do I do?

Where am I going?

Why am I motivated to do this?

Who am I?

When do I feel Adonai's favor?

6. It's time to write out your first identity statement draft. Remember, this is a *statement*. Don't use wording such as, "I want to become..." or "I will be..." as if they're things you still need to achieve, but rather, "I am..." with confidence. Even the things that you don't feel you're exhibiting perfectly in your life, state them in this way. You are calling out the character traits, personality, and

purpose Adonai has within you. It's there, no matter how small! Keep praying through this process, and listen for the Holy Spirit's direction. After you've written out the various callings, talents, and purposes you have, bring your identity statement to a close with, "I am (insert full name)" as a final declaration of who you are.

7.   Share your identity statement with someone who you
     know will give honest feedback. Ask them if they feel
     like your identity statement fits who you are. Is there
     something you should add, or something you should
     remove? Rework any changes.

8. Now is the time, beautiful and beloved daughter of Adonai! Write out your final identity statement and sign your name to it. Tape it to your wall, carry it in your purse, make it a part of who you are. Memorize it and speak it over yourself every day. It may not feel like you're living fully in all its power at times, but be patient. As you speak these truths over yourself, you will be amazed at how Elohim will manifest these callings and giftings in your life in a bold and powerful way!

This is who you are, my friend...and this is only the beginning of an incredible journey—a journey of living fully alive!

P. S.

I'm Praying For You

Dear Amazing You,

I wanted to add a little "P.S." before sending all these letters your way. I feel as though I've shared this amazing journey with you through every letter I've penned, and through every prayer I've prayed. I smile thinking of all the ways you've grown and changed as you've discovered more of Adonai's heart.

You are so covered in prayer.

Even as this book comes to a close, the journey is not over. We remain bonded together in Heavenly realms, spiritually linked eternally in Yeshua. Our identity in Him is a bridge that crosses all barriers and defines all things. Whether you live in the States or another country, whether you're living on the farm or have an urban studio apartment, there is no difference in Yeshua.

No matter where you are, I'm still cheering you on.

Seasons come and go. Spring turns to summer, and summer turns to fall. Throughout this season of letter writing, my porch swing was exchanged for a quiet corner in my local coffee shop, and the Queen Anne's lace disappeared under the snow. In all the changes around us, one thing never will change:

You are incredibly loved by Elohim.

You are so worthy of His love. Don't ever doubt it. He is passionately, crazy in love with the amazing, talented person who He created you to be. He is so eager to see you live a life fully alive, in a way that only you can, one choice at a time.

Go take the world by this Kingdom storm.

I hope you take this message of identity in Yeshua and share it everywhere you go—and that you set captives free from chains of insecurity. I hope you share what you've learned with your friends, and that you use this book as a tool for group studies and to speak words of life into your community. I hope you're brave and invite other people into your story, sharing the powerful testimony Adonai has written into your life. By doing so, I hope you create a sisterhood of women who confidently cheer one another on instead of comparing and compromising.

Knowing your identity in Yeshua changes everything.

Thank you for blessing my life by allowing me into yours. I'm praying you onwards to reach all the potential that is locked within your soul, and I am confident that Adonai will complete the good work He has started in your life.[1] You are fully equipped for the vision He has given to you.

For the Kingdom's sake and in Yeshua's love,

Victoria Humphrey

---

1.   Philippians 1:6

APPENDIX

Hosting a Study Group

Sometimes I get a wild fluttering in my heart, and I know that it's the Holy Spirit trying to get my attention. Maybe just reading the title of this appendix has your heart fluttering too—and if that's the case, I hope you keep reading!

You can do this!

If you feel like Adonai is asking you to start a study group using this book, I want you to know first and foremost that you are equipped for this (hello, chapter six!). I'm so excited that you are passionate about what Adonai has been teaching you through these pages, and that you want to share all you've learned with others!

You don't have to be perfect—just willing to allow others to join you on your journey.

You don't have to have everything mastered. You don't have to have the perfect answers. You don't even have to have the perfect Pinterest location or a home that is Instagram ready. All you have to do is ask Adonai who might need this message in their lives, and invite them into this story He is writing.

You just have to show up, and ask the Holy Spirit to show up, too.

It's really as simple as that! Don't underestimate what He can do with what you have. It doesn't need to be complicated, and you don't need to schedule every moment. All you need is a heart that is ready to both give and receive, and an atmosphere where the Holy Spirit is welcome to work in a mighty way.

You can be used by Elohim to break chains of bondage and to set His daughters free.

I want to give you some additional tools that I hope will give you more direction and spark new ideas as to how to put your own study group together. This is by no means an exhaustive list or a step-by-step guide on how you need to facilitate your group. This is just me, sharing some thoughts as we sit across from each other for coffee, excited to be dreaming with you about what Adonai could do in your life and in the lives of so many others!

INVITE: Ask Adonai who He would like to come join this study. Take time to be quiet in His presence, and let Him whisper some names to your heart. There are always the obvious people to invite—sisters, aunts, girlfriends, and the go-to women in your life—but who else might need this message? What about the girl in your congregation that always sits in the back row, the girl that no one really talks to? Or what about the widow who has no children and is often alone? Think beyond just peers to include both younger and older women, knowing that both have wisdom and insight to offer! Once you have your list of names and have prayed over them, go ahead and take the leap—send out a text message (or better yet, an actual invitation in the mail!) and ask them to join you for a weekly study! Be sure to include details on time, location, and where to purchase their own copy of the book. Give directions as to what sections you would like them to read beforehand, so they are prepared to come and share.

HOSTING: Again, you don't need to have a perfect location. It's less about how things look, and more about the atmosphere. You could have a beautiful home, but if the Holy Spirit is not present, you may find that no one opens up and your group is void of growth. Don't let less-than-ideal accommodations prevent you from opening up and sharing what you have! With that said, you do want things to be comfortable. Have your friends gather at a sunny kitchen table, or get cozy on the living room couches and floor (my preferred location!). You can also have soft worship music playing in the background to take the edge off of any silence as you wait for others to share.

FOOD: Serving food is entirely up to you, but it's a nice ice-breaker and tends to make people feel more at ease. Think of it as an opportunity to serve and feed your friends physically, in preparation for feeding their souls! I love doing a food bar with study groups—for example, I supply the main base item (such as hot chocolate), and then the guests are invited to bring toppings (such as whip cream, crushed peppermints, syrups, etc...). This gives everyone the opportunity to be involved in the kitchen together as you create your own dishes. Some other food bar ideas are ice cream sundaes, coffee and cookies, trail mix, baked potatoes, tacos, yogurt parfaits, and waffles/pancakes. You can also have theme snacks, such as everyone bringing their favorite cereal, or a favorite fruit to make a fruit salad together.

PRAYER: Start your group study with prayer, and invite Adonai to work powerfully in all of your lives. Let Him set the stage for all the sharing and growth that will happen! You can also extend the invitation at the end of your study time for prayer requests, before closing in prayer. As the leader, write down what each person shares, and be intentional to pray for them during the week.

STUDY: This book is set up in a way that makes sharing easy...if you're willing to be vulnerable! As the leader, you may have to be the one who shares things first in order to get the conversation flowing. You can start by asking what stood out in the chapter—maybe a specific sentence, paragraph, or concept jumped out and spoke to someone's heart. Then, you can just start going through the questions at the end of each chapter, inviting those present to share what they learned or how it impacted them. Realize that some of the questions are deep and personal, so not everyone may want to share—and that's alright! Be attentive to how the Holy Spirit guides your conversation. You may need to focus more on one specific question and end up skipping others because of lack of time. That's totally okay!

ACTIVITIES: Several chapters of this book have different activities, and it's up to you whether or not you'd like to do these together with your group, or individually throughout the week:

- *You Are Forgiven:* Create a mosaic using either pottery or paper.

- *You Are Beautiful:* Write a decorated reminder for your mirror with Psalm 139:14.

- *You Are Gifted:* Write a decorated reminder with Matthew 25:21

- *You Are An Overcomer:* Write (or paint!) a reminder that says "I am not common".

- *You Are Royalty:* Make a tiara/crown.

- *You Are Healed:* Decorate a gratitude journal.

- *You Are Beloved:* Create a ketubah—you could paint, draw, collage, etc.

- *You Are Free:* Create a bookmark with the prayer from the end of the chapter.

ACCOUNTABILITY: Throughout the days in between your group meetings, reach out to those in your group. Check in with them about how they're doing, and let them know that you're praying for them—especially if they've shared any specific prayer requests with you. Knowing that someone cares and is genuinely invested in their lives will cause them to want to stick with it! In addition, I would suggest having a mentor for yourself to keep you accountable, as well. Ask her to be praying for you as you lead this group, and feel free to ask her questions if you need wisdom on how to handle situations, too!

IDENTITY CELEBRATION: I would highly recommend that you host a special "identity celebration" at the end of your study! Invite everyone to dress up, and maybe even go out to dinner together or have a fun fondue party at your house. Go around the room and give each precious sister in your group the opportunity to stand up and share her identity statement aloud. When each one finishes, give her a loud round of applause and cheer of support! Celebrate each one's individuality, and the unique callings Adonai has on each of their lives.

Your group will be so special, so unique to those who are joining you. I'm here for each one of you, praying for you, and cheering you on!

Be strong and of good courage!

Acknowledgements & Thanks

Adonai, I am so overwhelmed by all You've done to bring me to this place. For birthing dreams in my heart, and being faithful to fulfill them in ways that only You could. I am so in awe of You. You romance my heart like no one else. The cry of my soul for this project was to have Your words. Take my small offerings, and make them enough. This is Your book, Your promises, Your heart. Do what You want with it. I am humbled to be a tool You choose to use.

Yeshua, no words can describe the depths of Your love. My heart is motivated by the cost of Your sacrifice. Thank you for seeing me as worthy, and as the one You want to pursue. I am so in love with You.

Mom and Dad, thank you for all that you've done to fuel the giftings Adonai has given me. Dad, you have equipped me to be bold in my faith and to walk according to the Holy Spirit's leading. I'm so blessed to be your daughter and to have your personality. Mom, the greatest gift you ever gave me was allowing me to write my own stories in 8th grade instead of following the textbook. You saw my talent and called it out. Thanks for letting me bend the rules and color outside the lines in a way that only I could. May I bring both of you honor and blessing all the days of your life.

To my grandparents: Your prayers over this project were manifested in powerful ways through the Holy Spirit. Your faith and encouragement are the greatest legacies and ones that I treasure with all my heart. Thank you for investing in my life.

To Sierra,[1] Katelyn, Marili, Gavi, Jennifer, Naomi, Hannah, Joy, and Cassie: The Holy Spirit is evident in your lives, and you are being used in mighty ways for the sake of the Kingdom. You have been given powerful testimonies that are filled with Adonai's glory. Thank you for entrusting me to share your stories. Keep being world changers!

Marili, thank you for being the voice I finally listened to. Your persistence in telling me to write a book finally paid off. If it wasn't for you, this book would still remain unwritten. Thanks for being amazing you. Let's travel the world, but make sure it leads back to Jerusalem!

Katelyn, your heart for identity in Yeshua defined my Israel trip in a life-changing way. I am so grateful to have you in my life. You are a woman of valor, and to watch you enter into this new season as a wife and mother has been a gift. Keep inspiring others, and bringing Heaven to earth.

To the Brumlows, Fourniers, Murphys, Autumn, Gram, Melanie, and Jennifer: Thank you for reading through my rough drafts. Your input and encouragement helped create what this book is today. I value your wisdom and friendship, and I am so grateful for each you. Putting my words into someone else's hands was scary, but your feedback made the process enjoyable.

Melanie, you were Adonai-sent. Our divine encounter in Texas was possibly the biggest gift God gave me towards this book. You took my words, saw my heart, and made me a better writer through your edification and critique. Thank you for everything, from the bottom of my heart.

Gram, you do everything with excellence. Not only did you spend hours editing, but you took the time to write

---

1.   Name changed

encouragement along with critiques. Your affirmations in the margins kept me from getting discouraged by the overwhelming process of making this draft into a book. Thank you for all your support, for speaking my love language, and for telling me, "I always knew you could do it!" You made the editing process a breeze, and I am so blessed to be your granddaughter. Let's celebrate in Israel!

Rebekah and Moriah, you've been my biggest cheerleaders in all the moments I desperately needed the extra push. The Father has showered His favor on me in extravagant ways through the two of you. There's no other duo I'd rather chase the Kingdom with—including continual WhatsApp message marathons and trekking across every Israeli vineyard. May we all dance together in the streets of Jerusalem soon!

To Messianic Jewish Publishers: I am so humbled and grateful for your support, enthusiasm, and patience. Thank you for seeing the potential in these pages, and for helping make my dreams a reality!

To all my nieces: This is my heart and prayer for you on these pages. There is nothing I desire more than for you to know the depth of Yeshua's love, and that you would know how desperately He wants your heart. May each of you know how much I love you as well—I'm always, always here for you. I can't wait to see how Adonai uses each of you in unique, original ways for the Kingdom's sake.